Partic

Deeper

Hearing God's Voice For Yourself and Others Through The Gift of Prophecy

Authored and Developed by

DEANNA OELKE

Published by Deeper Ministries
deeperministries@shaw.ca

Printed in USA

ISBN: 978-0-9952762-1-5

What Leaders Are Saying

"Prophecy wasn't new to me as I grew up in a context where it was taught and practiced – the good, bad and everything in between. I knew prophecy was a God given gift, but I found myself walking through long dormant seasons. I placed restrictions on myself believing a lie that I had to be in a charismatic environment in order to operate in this gifting. I was so very wrong. I craved community that understood the prophetic nature of the body of Christ. I found this from the first moment I met Deanna and journeyed through the Deeper experience. I received the most biblically sound teaching and practice of prophecy I had ever been exposed to. Deanna pulls from scripture, revelation and life experience. Her gift and wisdom take you on a journey of what it truly means to hear and obey the voice of God in a way that brings glory to God and exhorts others. The season spent with Deeper served as a catalyst in my life. This experience unlocked areas in my spiritual journey that had been closed for many years. I walked away equipped to disciple others to operate in a New Testament biblical approach to prophecy."

Travis Wilkins, Lead Pastor
Centre Street Church, Airdrie Campus (Airdrie, Alberta, Canada)

"If you've ever tried to tune in to a radio station from a remote location or watch television with rabbit ears you will understand static; scratchy, fuzzy sounds that distort and even cover up the picture or sound. My relationship with God was distorted by static. I was having trouble hearing God's voice. I was having trouble seeing his plans for me. The Deeper course gave me the space and tools to eliminate that static so my Heavenly Father's voice was clear. As a pastor, Deeper significantly enhanced my ministry by giving me the ability and confidence to use my prophetic voice to share God's love and encouragement with my friends and parishioners."

Jen Snow, Children and Families Pastor
Calgary First Church of the Nazarene (Calgary, Alberta, Canada)

"When invited to attend Deeper, I knew instantly that this was God's answer to my cry for help to learn about my spiritual gifts. Deanna is a strong pioneer who teaches with authenticity, vulnerability, wisdom and grace. She offers a perfect blend of solid biblical grounding with ample opportunity to practice exploring the gifts God has given to each of us. What struck me most profoundly through Deeper was the myriad of ways in which God bestows his gifts. It made me realize how vital it is for each of us in the body of Christ to operate in our giftedness. I encourage every believer to gather a few trusted people around you, and work your way through the Deeper materials together. I promise that you will grow in your appreciation and love of God, you will learn about who you are and what you specifically bring to the body of Christ. You will grow in confidence in living life more fully - being transformed and encouraged to press on."

Andrea Bye, Life Coach
Life on Purpose Coaching (Calgary, Alberta, Canada)

"In going through Deeper, I learned how to recognize, hear and test God's voice in a safe place. It was exciting to understand what I have been experiencing for years in communicating with God. Deeper has changed my life."

Valerie Hopman, Monday Night Evangelism
Centre Street Church (Calgary, Alberta, Canada)

"Deeper has dramatically changed my relationship with my Heavenly Father; it opened the door for a two-way communication with him. Hearing the voice of God for myself and others is a beautiful gift from above that is now a part of my everyday life. Not a day goes by that I don't hear, sense or feel His presence."

Regan Bowers, Replenish Ministry
Centre Street Church (Calgary, Alberta, Canada)

What Participants are Saying

"It is my great pleasure and honor to endorse Deanna's work with Deeper. Through the teaching in Deeper, the world of the prophetic came alive in my life. By celebrating the prophetic gift in me, Deeper taught me how to readily access and share Holy Spirit in a new and fresh way. My life and the lives of those around me have been deeply enriched."

Shari S.

"Hearing God's voice should be core doctrine in our churches. Deeper reinforced the biblical truth that God still speaks in a variety of ways, and it equipped me with "conversation starters" like entering his presence through worship and asking him specific questions. I was often amazed by how quickly, clearly and personally he answered. In living life, self-doubt can get in the way but there is nothing so reassuring as hearing and trusting God's voice. He speaks love that envelops me in tenderness, comfort and security. He is all I need and I want to know Him more."

Carolyn K.

"Deanna's teaching in Deeper has helped me take my relationship with God deeper and wider than I ever could have imagined. Learning to hear him speak to me and for others has been such a precious gift. It has enabled me to serve the body of Christ in new ways, and to walk closer with Him each and every day. Deanna and Deeper have been such incredible blessings in my life!"

Natalie D.

"Before I learned the principles taught in Deeper, I realize I had put God in a box. Learning how to engage with the Holy Spirit has transformed my relationship with Jesus Christ!"

Arienne C.

"I feel like my 'spiritual settings' have been adjusted and I can finally recognize the Holy Spirit speaking to me and showing me things. I guess I had been living in a two-dimensional world in the past with God the Father and Jesus, but now I can see the third dimension of this spiritual life with the Holy Spirit. The adventure has been amazing and I'm excited to walk each day with him!"

Teresa D.

"Deeper has transformed our family's relationships with God and with each other."

Ruth K.

"I was far from God and going through the motions when I came to Deeper. The worship provided an atmosphere for God to touch my life. As the weeks progressed I came to realize God wanted to speak to me and I was highly valued. The prophetic guidelines of comfort, encourage and strengthen made the place safe. The personal words from God through the prophetic gift from others touched me and broke the lies I believed about God."

Bill H.

"I have known Jesus as my personal savior for many years. For most of that time it never occurred to me that God wanted to, and already was, speaking to me. What a blessing to have Deanna's biblical teaching open my heart and ears to Holy Spirit's voice. What a joy to have a name for the sweet voice and presence that has been there through my journey and to become more fully aware of his role in my life. I am thankful for the help and guidance I received through Deeper as I continue in my spiritual journey."

Rachel B.

"I felt like a pioneer in my prophetic gifting. Deanna's teaching provided me with a solid biblical foundation for my journey in the prophetic. Deeper helped me recognize the variety of ways God speaks to encourage, comfort and strengthen myself and others and to thrive in God's Kingdom. After some practice, I noticed how energized I felt in my gift of prophecy as it demonstrated God's love in a relational way. My journey in the prophetic has greatly increased from Deanna's instruction and I look forward to more of her books!"

Kim B.

"Through Deeper, my relationship with Father God and Jesus Christ was beautifully transformed as I learned practical ways to abide in Jesus and enjoy his loving presence. I learned ways to truly listen to Holy Spirit. I discovered that not only has God been speaking to me all my life, but his written Word has opened up to me in amazing new ways. Praise God!"

Sophie I.

Dedications

I would like to dedicate this manual to my husband, Harvey, who modeled to me the faithful love of Father God. Thank you Harvey for giving me the freedom to pursue my healing and explore my identity. Your constant love, support and encouragement were instrumental for me to walk into my destiny. I believe this work is yours as well as mine and I thank God that he chose to bring you into my life. I am blessed beyond measure to journey with you in this adventure of life.

Acknowledgements

I would like to thank my pastor, Kervin Raugust, for his willingness to work with me on this manual. Kervin, thank you for investing your time not only in advising me and editing this manual but for contributing to my personal growth. I have never journeyed with someone that models living in the Word of God and in the Spirit of God as gracefully as you do. I count it a privilege to be under your leadership, mentorship and counsel.

Contents

Deeper - Part One

ENCOUNTER SESSION 1
Introduction & Core Principles

Trinity

"MAY THE GRACE OF THE LORD JESUS CHRIST, AND THE LOVE OF GOD AND THE FELLOWSHIP OF THE HOLY SPIRIT BE WITH YOU ALL." **2 CORINTHIANS 13:14**

THIS PAINTING SIMPLY CAPTURES THE TRINITY INTERACTING AS THE THREE IN ONE. FATHER GOD IS REPRESENTED BY THE HANDS, HOLY SPIRIT IS SYMBOLIZED AS CONSUMING FIRE, AND JESUS AS THE ROSE OF SHARON.

WWW.DEANNASDECORATIVEDESIGNS.CA

ORIGINAL ACRYLIC PAINTINGS AND PRINTS BY

DEANNA OELKE

Deeper—Encounter Session 1

Introduction & Core Principles

this is in line with new testament prophesy and is what we'll be learning more about.

Deeper is designed to be a prophetic community and a safe place to learn how to hear God's voice for oneself and for others, which is the gift of prophecy. The gift of prophecy will be taught in alignment with 1 Corinthians 14:3

"One who prophesies strengthens others, encourages them, and comforts them." (1 Cor. 14:3)

Opportunities will be provided to practice listening to God. The gift of prophecy and the spiritual gifts of 1 Corinthians 12 are given by Holy Spirit.

Deeper is also a place for you to discover and experience Holy Spirit. This can be done in isolation: one on one with you and Holy Spirit. At the same time, there is enrichment, acceleration and a depth in your relationship with Holy Spirit that can be experienced in biblical community. North American society values and esteems independence, but God does not. God values interdependence; he values us operating as the church in true and rich biblical community. Experiencing a rich, biblical prophetic community during our Deeper experience is our desire.

My prayer is that you will experience true biblical community in your Deeper experience. I pray that you will experience the church operating in Christ as a radiant church, without stain or wrinkle or any other blemish, but holy and blameless. (Eph. 5:27) I pray that this experience with Holy Spirit will spark a fire within you. I pray that you in turn will desire to partner with Holy Spirit in co-creating biblical community with others in your life.

The following are biblical principles that are foundational for our Deeper sessions.

our image of God is so important and it shapes our view of everything.

Principles of the Deeper Community

We believe God speaks:

"My sheep listen to my voice; I know them, and they follow me." (Jn. 10:27)

Deeper operates on the foundational understanding that as Christians, our spiritual inheritance is to hear the voice of God. The primary way that God speaks is through the written word of God – the Bible. God's spoken word is always lined up with the truth of the Bible and the character of God.

We believe that God can speak to us through others with the gift of prophecy:

"One who prophesies strengthens others, encourages them, and comforts them" (1 Cor. 14:3)

1 Corinthians 14:1-25 gives guidelines as to how the gift of prophecy is to be used. Prophecy in the Deeper community will be to strengthen, encourage and comfort others. These will be the guidelines that we follow as we learn to hear God's voice for others. This means that in delivering a prophetic word, we are not allowed to speak of what is wrong or point out sin in another person.

Love is our highest goal:

"Dear friends, let us continue to love one another, for love comes from God. Anyone who loves is a child of God and knows God." (1 Jn. 4:7)

God is love. All prophetic words will be rooted in the love nature of God. As we ask Father God what he loves about his children we begin to see each of them through his eyes of love. Prophetic words should be spoken from the heart of Father God for his children. As we learn about Holy Spirit, hear his voice, and practice operating in his gifts we want to be strategic in building a biblical prophetic community of love that will encourage each individual and support the work of Holy Spirit.

We believe sincerity of desire releases and increases our spiritual gifts:

"Let love be your highest goal! But you should also desire the special abilities the Spirit gives—especially the ability to prophesy." (1 Cor. 14:1)

As you see others in your Deeper group operating in their gift of prophecy, this may create a desire within you to have the gift as well. This scripture clearly states that we are to desire the gifts of Holy Spirit but especially the gift of prophecy. Think about the character of God: he is loving, kind, and a good Father who knows how to give good gifts. God would not have us desire the gift of prophecy and then withhold it from us. You may be coming into Deeper with the gift of prophecy, or you may not have the gift of prophecy and are coming because you desire to receive the gift of prophecy. Desire on your part is all that is needed to receive the gift of prophecy and to be a part of Deeper.

What will a Deeper Session Look Like?

Worship: Worship is core to the Deeper experience. Our worship times will provide opportunities for you to engage deeply with Father God, Jesus and Holy Spirit through:

- Singing
- Abiding/resting/waiting
- Meditating on God's Word
- Soaking in his presence

Freedom during worship is encouraged. You will have the freedom to worship God through a variety of expressions. Our goal during worship is to lavish our love on Jesus, Holy Spirt and Father God, and to connect deeply with them. Sometimes trying something different than what we are used to in worship helps us engage with God in a new or deeper way.

Teaching: The teaching of Deeper is biblically based and is designed to be easy for the leaders to teach, easy for you to learn and then easy for you to re-teach to your friends. A natural response of people within Deeper is to teach others the principles that have personally impacted them.

Deeper will be divided into 2 main parts:

Deeper – Part 1: Hearing God's Voice for Yourself

Lessons will include:

- Abiding
- Engaging with and Listening to Holy Spirit
- Ways that God Speaks
- Continuing to Grow in Hearing God's Voice
- Stewarding Truth
- Dreams

Deeper – Part 2: Hearing God's Voice for Others

Lessons will include:

- What is the Gift of Prophecy?
- Old and New Covenant Prophecy
- How to Give a Prophetic Word to Others
- Celebration and Prophetic Words
- How to Steward Prophetic Words that Others have Given to You
- Words of Wisdom & Words of Knowledge
- Glory Stories

Listening to God Exercises:

Deeper sessions will provide regular opportunities to practice hearing God's voice. Active involvement and engagement in each session is necessary. Deeper is not a 'sit back and learn' classroom setting, but rather a 'jump in and practice' experience. You will be risking and actively engaging in each session; when you engage, you will grow!

A Safe Community:

Every effort will be made to make Deeper a safe place to: learn, grow, risk, be yourself and make mistakes. You will have many opportunities to be vulnerable with the Deeper community as you share, participate in the listening exercises and learn to prophesy. Vulnerability is a choice. With love as our highest goal, can you risk sharing yourself with the people in this room? Hiding who you are is difficult in a community that learns to hear the voice of God. As we begin to practice the gift of prophecy, God will speak to others about what you need to hear from him. We will operate in the biblical standard for how the gift of prophecy should be used: in love, strengthening, encouraging and comforting (1 Cor. 13:2, 1 Cor. 14:3). No one will be allowed to point out sin or correct others with the gift of prophecy, for this is an abuse of the gift of prophecy and a violation of God's love nature.

Deeper - Part One

ENCOUNTER SESSION 2
Abiding in Jesus

Righteousness

"BLESSED ARE THOSE WHO HUNGER AND THIRST FOR RIGHTEOUSNESS, FOR THEY SHALL BE SATISFIED." MATTHEW 5:6

THE DICTIONARY DEFINES RIGHTEOUSNESS: "MORALLY UPRIGHT; WITHOUT GUILT OR SIN". AS CHRISTIANS, THIS SHOULD BE HOW WE WANT TO LIVE OUR LIVES. BUT, THE BIBLE SAYS THAT ALL OUR RIGHTEOUS ACTS ARE LIKE FILTHY RAGS! HOW THEN CAN I LIVE A RIGHTEOUS LIFE WITHOUT SIN? THE KEY IS JESUS CHRIST AND THE POWER OF THE CROSS: LIVING IN JESUS AND JESUS LIVING IN ME.

WWW.DEANNASDECORATIVEDESIGNS.CA
ORIGINAL ACRYLIC PAINTINGS AND PRINTS BY
DEANNA OELKE

Worship Reflections

Journal, Draw, Doodle

Deeper—Encounter Session 2

Abiding in Jesus

Another word that is used in Bible translations for abide is 'remain'. Remain in Jesus. Abiding or remaining in Jesus means to be in connected relationship with Jesus.

The principle and practice of abiding in Jesus is important for teaching you to tune your spirit to the Spirit of God. Abiding then becomes a pathway in learning to hear God's voice. Often many Christians already have learned how to abide in Jesus but do not articulate it as abiding. People who are worshippers often naturally engage in a posture of abiding within a worship setting. Abiding is meant to be a lifestyle posture within Jesus not an event or experience. Abiding is something that you practice on a regular basis so that you can then learn how to commune continuously with the Lord.

Before we learn about abiding I want to distinguish between spirit, soul and body. We are made up of three parts: body (which is our physical body), soul (our mind, will, and emotions), and our spirit (the truest part of who we are). Some scriptures and preachers use the term soul and spirit interchangeably. These following scriptures make a clear distinction between the soul and the spirit.

"May God himself, the God of peace, sanctify you through and through. May your whole <u>spirit, soul and body</u> be kept blameless at the coming of our Lord Jesus Christ." (1 Thess. 5:23 NIV)

For the word of God is alive and powerful. It is sharper than the sharpest two-edged sword, cutting between <u>soul and spirit</u>, between joint and marrow. It exposes our innermost thoughts and desires." (Heb. 4:12)

For the teaching in Deeper, I will use the term soul and spirit in the following ways:

Our Spirit:

Our spirit is the truest part of who we are, is eternal and will continue living on once our bodies have died. Our spirit is what makes us distinctly different from animals and is how we are uniquely made in the image of God (Gen. 1:27). God is spirit (Jn. 4:24a). When he created Adam and Eve in the Garden of Eden with a spirit, they had a spirit connection with God and had the ability to commune and talk with God. When Adam and Eve sinned, they lost spiritual connection with God. Jesus has made it possible to be born again of God's spirit (Eph. 2:4-5, 1 Cor. 5:17). Through the death and resurrection of Jesus Christ we can re-establish a spiritual connection with God.

Our Soul:

"He restores my soul; he leads me in the paths of righteousness for His name's sake." (Ps. 23:3 NKJV)

Our soul is our mind, our will and our emotions. Your soul is where pain, rejection, fear, hurts and past memories are. David in this Psalm states that our soul needs to be restored; our soul is not born again. Some of the ways that our souls can be restored is through obeying the truth by God's Spirit (1Pet. 1:22-23) and by renewing our mind (Rom. 12:2). Restoring our soul is an ongoing process.

_____

_____

_____

_____

_____

_____

_____

Worshiping God and Engaging our Spirit

"But the time is coming—indeed it's here now—when true worshipers will worship the Father in spirit and in truth. The Father is looking for those who will worship him that way. For God is Spirit, so those who worship him must worship in spirit and in truth." (Jn. 4:23-24)

God, Jesus, and Holy Spirit are spirit beings, and we commune and worship them with our spirits. Similarly, abiding in Jesus is our spirit remaining within the Spirit of Jesus, and the Spirit of Jesus remaining within our spirit. Worship can be a time to practice how to abide in Jesus. The principle and practice of abiding helps us tune into how our spirit communes with the Spirit of Jesus and then how God speaks to us. Holy Spirit is available to help us in this.

Worship at Deeper will also be a time to practice how to abide in Jesus. Before we learn how to abide, let's read and reflect on the following invitation from Jesus to abide in him.

"I am the true vine, and my Father is the gardener. [2] He cuts off every branch in me that bears no fruit, while every branch that does bear fruit he prunes so that it will be even more fruitful. [3] You are already clean because of the word I have spoken to you. [4] Remain in me, as I also remain in you. No branch can bear fruit by itself; it must remain in the vine. Neither can you bear fruit unless you remain in me."

[5] "I am the vine; you are the branches. If you remain in me and I in you, you will bear much fruit; apart from me you can do nothing. [6] If you do not remain in me, you are like a branch that is thrown away and withers; such branches are picked up, thrown into the fire and burned. [7] If you remain in me and my words remain in you, ask whatever you wish, and it will be done for you. [8] This is to my Father's glory, that you bear much fruit, showing yourselves to be my disciples."

[9] "As the Father has loved me, so have I loved you. Now remain in my love. [10] If you keep my commands, you will remain in my love, just as I have kept my Father's commands and remain in his love." (Jn. 15:1-10 NIV)

What are some of the spiritual truths, commands, and promises that you hear from this passage on abiding in Jesus?

_____

_____

_____

_____

_____

_____

_____

_____

_____

_____

_____

_____

_____

_____

Why does Jesus teach this concept of abiding in him and in his love? Listen to his explanation:

¹¹"I have told you this so that my joy may be in you and that your joy may be complete. ¹²My command is this: Love each other as I have loved you. ¹³Greater love has no one than this: to lay down one's life for one's friends. ¹⁴You are my friends if you do what I command. ¹⁵I no longer call you servants, because a servant does not know his master's business. Instead, I have called you friends, for everything that I learned from my Father I have made known to you. ¹⁶You did not choose me, but I chose you and appointed you so that you might go and bear fruit—fruit that will last—and so that whatever you ask in my name the Father will give you. ¹⁷This is my command: Love each other." (Jn. 15:11-17 NIV)

Can you hear Jesus' intention in his invitation to abiding? That you would have intimate <u>friendship</u> with him!

Abiding in Jesus, remaining in his love and being his friend requires applying energy to the relationship and obedience on our part.

"If you keep my commands, you will remain in my love." (Jn. 15:10a NIV)

"You are my friends if you do what I command." (Jn. 15:14 NIV)

Obedience to God is obeying him in our words and our actions and it is a submissive posture on our part. A submissive posture of surrender and obedience is saying, 'yes' with all of who we are to all of who God is. The same is true of abiding in Jesus. Abiding in Jesus is simply saying 'yes' to Jesus with every part of our being. Remember our being is made up of three parts: spirit, soul (mind, will, emotions) and body.

Most Christians have experienced a time in their relationship with Jesus when they feel very close to him, and experienced the result of abiding in their body, soul (mind, will, emotions) and spirit. You may have sensed Jesus' presence in a very tangible way, felt his presence and love invade your emotions, and felt a deep spirit to spirit connection with your friend, Jesus.

The Practice of Abiding:

The posture of abiding is simply saying 'yes' to Jesus with your spirit, soul (mind, will, emotions), and your body. This is a practical way that you can posture your spirit to abide in the Spirit of Jesus before you enter into a time of worship, devotions, or an intentional time with him. When you know how to abide, you can practice it more quickly and easily and learn to live in the posture of abiding. Sometimes you may feel the presence of Jesus and see fruit quickly. Sometimes you won't see the fruit quickly; sometimes it grows with time. Don't rely on your emotions or physical sensations as an indication of abiding. If you are coming to Jesus in a posture of submission and obedience, choose to believe by faith that your spirit is abiding in the Spirit of Jesus. Sometimes Jesus wants to teach us to come to him by faith and not rely on our emotions or other parts of our being. The key is in resting, trusting, expecting, anticipating and waiting on him.

Satan does not want us to abide in Jesus and bear much fruit. He will do whatever he can to draw us out of this posture. Often he does this by hooking into our soul and distracting us through our feelings or mind. This is where obedience is necessary to remain in a place of abiding.

Examples:

- Satan may try to stir anxiety in you related to a situation. You can chose to not be anxious, and instead come to Jesus and say 'yes' with your body, soul and spirit. From this place of abiding, present the situation to Jesus. Ask him to speak truth into the situation, ask him to provide you with a verse to fight against the anxiety. Speak this verse out loud. Allow the peace of Jesus to flood your spirit, soul and body (Phil. 4:6-7).
- Satan may try to plant thoughts of doubt that are contrary to the Word of God. Instead of thinking about the logic of the thought, take the thought captive and come into a posture of abiding. Ask Jesus for a truth of his Word that directly fights this thought of doubt. Speak this truth out loud. (2 Cor. 10:4-5)

These are two practical examples of how positioning your spirit to abide in the Spirit of Jesus can be used in daily life. Learning to abide in Jesus can become a constant and consistent posture from which we live our Christianity.

_____

_____

_____

_____

_____

_____

_____

_____

_____

_____

_____

_____

_____

_____

_____

_____

_____

Listening Exercise

The Practice of Abiding

We are now going to practice abiding in Jesus.

Consciously choose to engage the following parts of your being with Jesus:

Your body: Choose a body posture that says 'yes' to Jesus.

Your soul:

- Your will: Choose to say 'yes' to Jesus. Choose to trust him.
- Your mind: Say 'yes', in your mind and then out loud to Jesus.
- Your emotions: Say 'yes' to Jesus with your feelings or your heart.

Your spirit: Your spirit is the truest part of who you are. From the depths of your being, your spirit, communicate a 'yes' to Jesus and all that he is.

Going Deeper – Extra Practice

Living in Abiding

What would it be like if you chose to say 'yes' to Holy Spirit, Father God and Jesus with all of who you are every moment of the day?

If this is your desire, the following is a prayer that you can pray regularly:

"Father, I choose to be a spiritual woman/man of God. I desire to walk all the days of my life in Holy Spirit. In Jesus' name, I command my body, mind, will and emotions to submit to my spirit, and I command my spirit to submit to Holy Spirit of mighty Jehovah God. I choose to receive no strength, help, support or guidance from any other spirit other than the Holy Spirit of God in Jesus' name. Amen."

Practice engaging your whole being: body, soul, and spirit with Jesus before you have your personal times with God. The more you practice saying 'yes' to Jesus with all parts of who you are, the easier this will get. Practice engaging with Holy Spirit, Father God and Jesus throughout the day, and especially when you engage with other people.

At the end of your devotional time or the end of your day, reflect on what this was like. As you were abiding, did you sense any fruit of Holy Spirit? Did you sense his presence? Was he speaking to you? Journal with Holy Spirit, Father God and Jesus about your times with him or your day with him.

Deeper - Part One

ENCOUNTER SESSION 3
Engaging With Holy Spirit

"THE SPIRIT OF THE SOVEREIGN LORD IS ON ME, BECAUSE THE LORD HAS ANOINTED ME TO PROCLAIM GOOD NEWS TO THE POOR. HE HAS SENT ME TO BIND UP THE BROKEN HEARTED, TO PROCLAIM FREEDOM FOR THE CAPTIVES AND RELEASE FROM DARKNESS FOR THE PRISONERS." ISAIAH 61:1 (NIV)

BEFORE PAINTING THIS PICTURE, GOD HAD BEEN SPEAKING TO ME SO OFTEN ABOUT BUTTERFLIES. AS I QUESTIONED HIM, I REALIZED THAT HE WANTED TO SPEAK TO ME ABOUT FREEDOM. JESUS HAS THE POWER TO TRANSFORM A LIFE. AS THIS TRANSFORMATION TAKES PLACE, THERE IS SUCH NEW FOUND FREEDOM TO BE BEAUTIFULLY AUTHENTIC! IN THIS PAINTING THE WOMAN IS AWARE OF THE TRANSFORMATION AND BEAUTY THAT IS TAKING PLACE WITHIN HER, BUT HER ATTENTION REMAINS FIXED ON HER FIRST LOVE: JESUS CHRIST.

WWW.DEANNASDECORATIVEDESIGNS.CA
ORIGINAL ACRYLIC PAINTINGS AND PRINTS BY
DEANNA OELKE

Worship Reflections

Journal, Draw, Doodle

Deeper—Encounter Session 3
Engaging With Holy Spirit

We all come into spiritual communities with our ideas and experiences about Father God, Jesus and Holy Spirit. We often come with a God box. Similarly, the Jews had ideas about the promised Messiah. Jesus ended up looking very different then what they expected. Before Jesus' ascension, he reminds his believers that the promised Holy Spirit would be coming. The believers likely had ideas about Holy Spirit and what he would be like.

Let's read about the believers' introduction to Holy Spirit in the book of Acts:

The Holy Spirit Comes

"On the day of Pentecost all the believers were meeting together in one place. Suddenly, there was a sound from heaven like the roaring of a mighty windstorm, and it filled the house where they were sitting. Then, what looked like flames or tongues of fire appeared and settled on each of them. And everyone present was filled with the Holy Spirit and began speaking in other languages, as the Holy Spirit gave them this ability." (Acts 2:1-4

Reflect as a group:

How did Holy Spirit make himself known to the believers on the day of Pentecost?

This was a powerful, experiential, supernatural encounter that they had with Holy Spirit. What are some of your feelings when you think about having a powerful, experiential, supernatural encounter with Holy Spirit? Why?

Often Christians are concerned and cautious about having spiritual experiences. Why do you think this is?

What do you know about Holy Spirit? Who is he personally to you? How is he different or the same as Father God and Jesus?

_____

_____

_____

_____

_____

_____

_____

_____

_____

_____

_____

Bible Verses About the Activity of Holy Spirit:

Teaches:

"But when the Father sends the Advocate as my representative—that is, the Holy Spirit—he will teach you everything and will remind you of everything I have told you." (Jn. 14:26)

"For the Holy Spirit will teach you at that time what needs to be said." (Luke 12:12)

Gives Life:

"The Spirit alone gives eternal life. Human effort accomplishes nothing. And the very words I have spoken to you are spirit and life." (John 6:63)

Intercedes:

"And the Holy Spirit helps us in our weakness. For example, we don't know what God wants us to pray for. But the Holy Spirit prays for us with groanings that cannot be expressed in words." (Rom. 8:26)

Filled by:

"And everyone present was filled with the Holy Spirit and began speaking in other languages, as the Holy Spirit gave them this ability." (Acts 2:4)

_____

_____

_____

_____

_____

Holy Spirit may be calling you to a deeper place of surrender and trust in who he is, his ways, and the work that he desires to do within you. Whatever your relationship with Holy Spirit is like, there is always a greater depth you can go. If you desire a deeper relationship with Holy Spirit express this desire to him. If you have concerns, confess these to him as well. If you recognize that you have a God box, surrender your box to him. Express your trust in him and who he is, and his ways.

_____

_____

_____

_____

_____

_____

_____

_____

_____

_____

_____

_____

_____

Engaging With & Listening to Holy Spirit

As we engage with Holy Spirit and listen to him, we want to take the posture of abiding: our spirits engaging with the Spirit of God. This posture is one of openness and submission to Father God, Jesus and Holy Spirit. This posture allows us to be sensitive to any way that Holy Spirit may choose to engage with us; we are postured for Holy Spirit to invade our space.

The posture of abiding can also be more active on our part. As we intentionally listen to Holy Spirit, we can press into him, his voice and ensure that we are receiving all that he wants to give us; we can invade his space.

Reflect on these verses from Romans 8:

"And the Holy Spirit helps us in our weakness. For example, we don't know what God wants us to pray for. But the Holy Spirit prays for us with groanings that cannot be expressed in words. And the Father who knows all hearts knows what the Spirit is saying, for the Spirit pleads for us believers in harmony with God's own will. And we know that God causes everything to work together for the good of those who love God and are called according to his purpose for them." (Rom. 8:26-28)

If we ask Holy Spirit what he is praying for us, we simply need to pray in agreement and cooperate with the work that he wants to do to fulfill God's will. We can ask Holy Spirit at any time what he is praying to Father God on our behalf. This can be particularly beneficial upon entering into new seasons (New Year, new job, ministry, etc.).

_____

_____

_____

Preparing to Actively Listen to Holy Spirit

We hear/sense/perceive from three different sources: ourselves, God, and Satan. As we prepare to hear the voice of God, we can pray to ensure that it is God's voice that we are listening to:

1. Through the name of Jesus, we can silence the voice of Satan: "In the name of Jesus, I silence the voice of any spirits that are contrary to Holy Spirit."

2. As we prepare our spirit, soul (mind/imagination, will, emotions,) and body to hear God's voice, we pray a prayer of submission. We do not turn ourselves 'off'; God can speak through all parts of our being when he speaks to our spirit: "I joyfully submit my spirit, soul, and body to you, Holy Spirit."

3. Our imagination/mind is one way that God speaks to us. Sometimes we are exposed to images, sounds and experiences that 'dirty' our imagination and interfere with hearing and seeing from God. Ask Jesus to clean your imagination. Ask him to forgive you, if necessary, and to wash away all of the un-holy things you have seen, heard, or experienced.

4. As you ask Holy Spirit questions, by faith choose to believe that the words, thoughts, pictures, images, senses that you have are from him: "I welcome you Holy Spirit to speak to me, I declare that I am God's child and I hear his voice."

When you are beginning to hear Holy Spirit's voice, it is easiest to start by asking him questions. When you ask him a question, write down what you sense/hear/perceive that he is saying. Keep writing until you sense that he is done 'speaking'. Ask him more questions about what he has said to you. Ensure that you have heard everything from Holy Spirit.

As you are listening, ensure that your mind stays submitted to your spirit. It is very easy for your mind to stop the flow of Holy Spirit speaking. Take the approach that you are receiving a dictation; purely write what you are hearing.

After you sense that Holy Spirit is done speaking, then rely on your mind to discern what you have written and ensure that it lines up with the truth of the Bible and the character of God.

When listening to Holy Spirit, sometimes you know immediately that it is Holy Spirit speaking. In these moments, it is easy to receive the words from Holy Spirit. But, sometimes it is not obvious and the dictation that you wrote down feels more like yourself. A common question in these encounters is: "How do I know if it is my voice or Holy Spirit's voice?" If it is your voice and what you received is in line with the Bible and with the character of God, then at the very least you are encouraging yourself in 100% of your own power! There is no harm in this; we all have 'encouraged ourselves'. If Holy Spirit was speaking, you will see fruit at a level that is greater than self-encouragement (love, truth, life, and fruit of the Spirit). Sometimes it is only with time that you see the fruit of Holy Spirit speaking. If, with time, you see fruit and you realize it was God's voice, remember what it was like when you received this word from the Lord. This will help you in tuning in to how he speaks to you.

Remember: God's voice is pure and holy, and will never contradict the Bible, or his character.

_____

_____

_____

_____

_____

_____

_____

_____

Listening Exercise

The Story of Jesus and Peter Walking on Water (Matt. 14:22-32)

Imagine yourself in the story of Jesus and Peter...

- Sitting in the boat, fighting the waves.
- Seeing Jesus walk towards you.
- Being called by Jesus.
- Choosing faith instead of doubt to walk to Jesus.

As you are in the boat obediently going where Jesus has asked you to go, who or what is fighting you?

_____

_____

_____

_____

_____

_____

_____

_____

_____

_____

What emotions or fears do you sense rising up within you?

_____

_____

_____

_____

_____

_____

_____

_____

As you choose faith and walk towards Jesus in a new way, what doubts or fears distract you from walking towards Jesus?

_____

_____

_____

_____

_____

_____

_____

_____

Hear Jesus ask you, "Why did you doubt me?" What do you say in response?

_____

_____

_____

_____

_____

_____

_____

_____

_____

_____

Listen to Jesus' response to your doubt. What truth is Jesus giving you about himself that will combat this doubt?

_____

_____

_____

_____

_____

_____

_____

_____

_____

_____

_____

_____

_____

_____

_____

_____

_____

_____

Speak out loud this truth about who Jesus is each time you feel or hear the voice of doubt want to distract you from moving toward Jesus in a new way.

Going Deeper – Extra Practice

Invite Holy Spirit into your time.

Pray the following prayer to prepare yourself to hear God's voice:

"In the name of Jesus, I silence the voice of any spirits that are contrary to Holy Spirit. I joyfully submit my spirit, soul, imagination, and body to you, Holy Spirit. I welcome you, Holy Spirit, to speak to me, and I declare that I am God's child and I hear his voice."

Now that we have prepared ourselves to hear God's voice, let's begin our listening exercise. As you ask Holy Spirit the questions, choose to engage your faith and believe that the first things that you see or hear are coming from Holy Spirit. Begin writing as you have thoughts, impressions, or pictures. Continue to press your spirit into the Spirit of the Lord (posture of abiding) to ensure that you are receiving all the information that he wants to give you about each question. After you have written answers from all of the questions, then go back and read what you have written. Ensure that what you have written lines up with the Bible and the character of God.

"But the Holy Spirit prays for us with groanings that cannot be expressed in words. And the Father who knows all hearts knows what the Spirit is saying, for the Spirit pleads for us believers in harmony with God's own will." (Rom. 8:26-27)

As I enter into this Deeper adventure, what are you praying for me Holy Spirit?

_____

_____

_____

_____

_____

_____

_____

_____

_____

_____

_____

What do you want to teach me about yourself?

_____

_____

_____

_____

_____

_____

_____

_____

What do you want to teach me about myself?

_____

_____

_____

_____

_____

_____

_____

_____

_____

What do you want to teach me within this community?

_____

_____

_____

_____

_____

_____

_____

What excites you about my place in the Deeper community?

_____
_____
_____
_____
_____
_____
_____
_____

How can I cooperate with you, Holy Spirit, for God's will to be accomplished in my life during my Deeper Experience?

_____
_____
_____
_____
_____
_____
_____
_____

Now that you are finished listening to Holy Spirit, go back and read what you have written and ensure that what you have received lines up with the Bible and the character of God.

Deeper - Part One

Hearts on Fire

"OUR HEARTS WERE BURNING WITHIN US WHILE HE TALKED WITH US."
LUKE 24:32 (NIV)

AFTER CO-FOUNDING A PROPHETIC MINISTRY (HEARTS ON FIRE MINISTRIES), I
WAS SEEKING THE LORD FOR A PAINTING THAT WOULD CAPTURE THE ESSENCE OF
OUR MINISTRY. I WAS WORSHIPPING ONE NIGHT WHEN I SAW, IN VISION, A
FLAMING HEART WITH THE FLAMES FORMING A WOMAN WORSHIPPING. THE
VISION CAPTURED OUR MINISTRY PERFECTLY.

WWW.DEANNASDECORATIVEDESIGNS.CA
ORIGINAL ACRYLIC PAINTINGS AND PRINTS BY
DEANNA OELKE

Worship Reflections

Journal, Draw, Doodle

Deeper—Encounter Session 4

Ways That God Speaks

This session of Deeper will look at different ways God speaks. Hearing about different ways that God speaks can create an openness and a desire within us for hearing God in new ways. As we explore the variety of ways that God can speak to his people, we need to remember that one way is not more valid than another. The subtle voice of God is just as valid as the audible voice of God; one just requires more faith on our part. God chooses <u>how</u> he speaks to us, we just need to receive and accept the way he chooses, and if necessary engage our faith to believe that he is speaking.

"And it is impossible to please God without faith. Anyone who wants to come to him must believe that God exists and that he rewards those who sincerely seek him." (Heb. 11:6)

Choosing to engage faith is a vital part of growing in hearing God's voice. Faith should be a constant companion in our spiritual journey. The goal in learning to hear God's voice is relationship with him. As you listen to God in the exercises, choose faith that God will draw near to you as you draw near to him, believe that he desires to speak to you and come expecting to hear his voice.

The following is a list of some of the ways that God could choose to speak to you. Sometimes God will begin speaking to you in a new way once you are open to possibilities.

If you think that God may be trying to speak to you through one of the following ways, do not dismiss it. Pay attention and start asking God questions.

Bible:

This is the primary way that God speaks to us. What a privilege that we can pick up the Word of God at any time to receive encouragement, comfort, and wise counsel. All other ways that God speaks must be weighed against the truth of God's written Word.

_____

_____

_____

_____

Audible Voice:

Clearly and audibly hear the voice of God. God's audible voice usually sounds like it is coming from an external source (outside of your mind or body).

_____

_____

_____

_____

Still Small Voice:

This often feels like your thoughts, and it sounds like it is coming from within your mind or body. Pay attention to random thoughts or people that pop into your head. Instead of disregarding them, press into the Lord and ask him if he is trying to communicate with you.

_____

_____

_____

_____

Visions:

Open Eye Vision:

Eyes are open and you see a vision at the same time you see the natural.

_____

_____

_____

_____

Closed Eye Vision:

Eyes are closed and you see a picture.   This feels more like your imagination.

_____

_____

_____

_____

Open Eye Spiritual Vision:

Eyes are open but you see the picture in your spirit. This may feel more like an impression. You may not see the picture clearly, but you know what it is.

_____

_____

_____

_____

Through Feelings:

As you are engaging with God, pay attention to feelings that you may suddenly have. Sometimes God shares his feelings with you that he has about situations or other people. Does your heart fill with love as you think about someone? Do you suddenly feel sad? Press into God and ask him more questions about what you are feeling.

_____

_____

_____

Through Impressions:

This is a very subtle way that God can speak. It is like a mix of a thought and a feeling, but not as clear.

_____

_____

_____

Through Your Body:

How does your body physically respond in God's presence, or to God's truth? Sometimes God wants to highlight something that is said, and may give you a physical sensation (shivers, burning sensation, etc.). Sometimes God may want you to act on something that he is telling you, and may give you a physical sensation to encourage you that it is him (butterflies in your stomach).

_____

_____

_____

Symbols in the Natural World (nature, objects, time on the clock, etc.):

Pay attention when something catches your eye, or when you see something over and over again. This could be God trying to communicate with an object. Often he uses objects in a symbolic way.

_____

_____

_____

Clothes That Someone is Wearing:

People often dress how they feel. This is especially true for women. Often, without realizing it, they sense something that is happening in their spirit, and they dress accordingly. When someone's clothing or jewelry catches your attention, start asking God questions; this may be the start of a prophetic word for them.

_____

_____

_____

Through Other Believers:

Whenever anyone speaks to you with an encouraging message from the Lord, receive the words and then take the words to God. Holy Spirit is the expert on you and your life. Use the Bible and Holy Spirit to discern the truth of the word.

_____

_____

_____

Colours:

Colours are symbolic and have certain meanings. If you are sensing or seeing colours, ask God what the colours symbolize.

_____

_____

_____

Dreams:

Not all dreams are spiritual dreams. When you sense that a dream is from God, journal it, and press into Holy Spirit to see what it means. Share your dreams with trusted prophetic friends and ask if they have an interpretation. We will be discussing dreams and dream interpretation more in depth later in Deeper. In the meantime, pray that God will speak to you through dreams.

_____

_____

_____

Angelic Visitation:

You may begin to have visions of angels, see angels in your dreams, or feel the presence of an angel. If you encounter an angel, make Jesus your default. Ask Jesus questions about the angel instead of dialoguing directly with the angel.

_____

_____

_____

Other Ways That God Speaks:

_____

_____

_____

_____

As you are exploring different ways that God may want to speak to you, relax and have fun! The focus here is on relationship with God; enjoy your time with him. If hearing God's voice does not seem to be coming easily for you, keep practicing. Don't become discouraged! Remember that the Bible is the primary way that God speaks to his children. Communing with God through his written word, the Bible, is full of rewards and builds relationship with him.

As you are in your Deeper community and others share what they sense that God is saying, it is common to think that how someone else hears from God is grander than how you hear from God. Often this is because we have grown accustomed to the subtlety of hearing God's voice for ourselves, and may have dismissed it numerous times. Begin to tune in to the subtle ways that God may be speaking to you; grab onto the gentle whispers and engage with God to see what else he may want to say.

Listening Exercise
Exploring Ways that God Speaks

The following listening exercise will encourage you to engage with God and receive from him in a variety of ways. Some ways may feel very awkward and some may feel very natural for you. Jump around the list and try ones that you like first. Try as many as you have time for. Most of all have fun and enjoy your time with God, Jesus and Holy Spirit!

Pray the following prayer to prepare yourself to hear God's voice:

"In the name of Jesus, I silence the voice of any spirits that are contrary to Holy Spirit. I joyfully submit my spirit, soul, imagination, and body to you, Holy Spirit. I welcome you Holy Spirit to speak to me, I declare that I am God's child and I hear his voice."

As you ask God, Jesus or Holy Spirit the following questions, engage your faith and trust that the first thing that you see, hear, sense is from God, and then ask more questions. Be curious! Remember, when you are done listening, to line up what you received with the Bible and the character of God.

Bible:

Ask Jesus what Bible verse he would like to speak to you. Why did he choose this verse for you?

_____

_____

_____

_____

Audible Voice or Still Small Voice:

Ask God to speak in your thoughts, a still small voice or an audible voice. Ask him to remind you of a childhood memory. In your mind remember the details of this memory. Ask God what he would like to say to you about this memory.

_____

_____

_____

_____

Visions:
Engage your imagination and ask God to show you his heart. What does it look like?

_____

_____

_____

_____

Ask him to show you something in his heart that you need.

_____

_____

_____

_____

Why do you need this part of his heart?

_____

_____

_____

_____

Through Feelings:

Target where you feel your emotions. Ask Holy Spirit to give you a feeling that he has right now. Can you articulate what the feeling is?

_____

_____

_____

_____

Ask him questions about this feeling of his: is it for a situation or a person? Is there something that he wants to say regarding his feeling that he is sharing with you? Is there something that he wants you to do?

_____

_____

_____

_____

Through Impressions:

This is a very subtle way that God can speak. It is like a mix of a thought and a feeling, but not as clear. Ask God to impress on you what he loves about you.

_____

_____

_____

_____

Why does he love this about you?

_____

_____

_____

_____

Symbols in the Natural world (nature, objects, time on the clock, etc.):

Ask God to highlight something in the room. What does he want to say to you about this object?

_____

_____

_____

_____

Clothes That Someone is Wearing:

Ask God to highlight something that someone is wearing: clothes, jewelry, etc. Why is he highlighting this?

_____

_____

_____

_____

Is there something that he wants to say to this person?

_____

_____

_____

_____

Colours:

Ask Holy Spirit to show you a colour. What does this colour mean? What does he want to say to you regarding this colour?

_____

_____

_____

_____

Going Deeper—Extra Practice

Engaging with the Trinity

The Trinity is three in one. They are each very distinct and different, yet the same. As you engage with each of them separately, you will begin to develop a relationship with each of them and with all of them. Practice engaging with Father God, Jesus and Holy Spirit as they lead you in your devotions, Bible reading, and as you do life. Invite them individually into different parts of your day. The focus is relationship here – enjoy life with them!

Engaging with ways that God speaks

Continue to engage with Father God, Jesus, and Holy Spirit to discover different ways that they want to communicate with you. If you didn't finish Exploring Ways that God Speaks listening exercise from Deeper, then complete it now. Try engaging ways and ask God other questions about yourself and about situations in your life. Try engaging with God and as you go about your day.

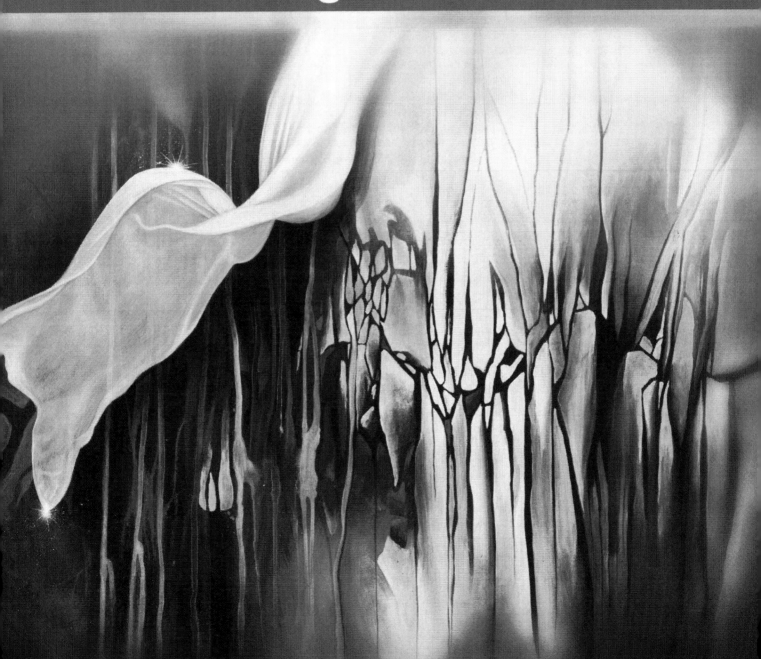

Deeper - Part One

ENCOUNTER SESSION 5
Continuing to Grow in Hearing God's Voice

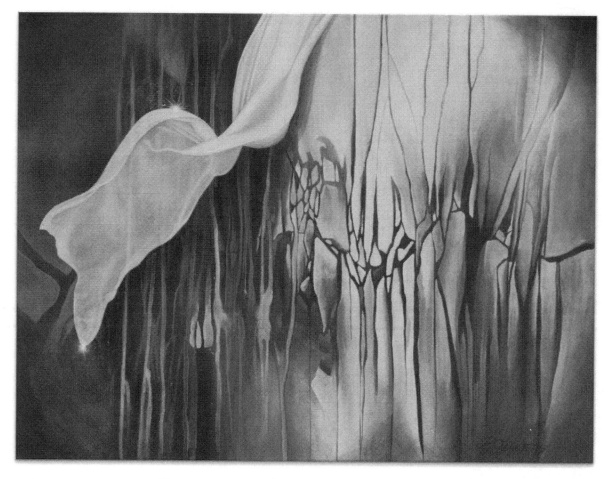

Garment of Praise

"(JESUS GAVE ME) THE GARMENT OF PRAISE FOR THE SPIRIT OF HEAVINESS." ISAIAH 61:3 (NKJV)

THIS PAINTING IS THE THIRD IN A SERIES ON ISAIAH 61. THE BACKGROUND ALLUDES TO BROKENNESS AND HEAVINESS THAT HAS PENETRATED THE BODY, SOUL AND SPIRIT. THE FABRIC REPRESENTS THE GARMENT OF PRAISE; THE ANTIDOTE FOR THE BURDENED, FAILING SPIRIT.

GOD HAS MADE EVERYTHING BEAUTIFUL IN ITS TIME (ECCL. 3:11). WHEN WE ALLOW JESUS TO TOUCH THE SPIRIT OF HEAVINESS AND WORK WITHIN US, WE CAN'T HELP BUT BE TRANSFORMED. THE RESULTS ARE BEYOND WHAT WE COULD DO IN OUR OWN HUMAN STRENGTH – THE RESULTS ARE SUPERNATURAL.

WWW.DEANNASDECORATIVEDESIGNS.CA
ORIGINAL ACRYLIC PAINTINGS AND PRINTS BY
DEANNA OELKE

Worship Reflections

Journal, Draw, Doodle

Deeper—Encounter Session 5

Continuing to Grow in Hearing God's Voice

"Come close to God, and God will come close to you." (Jas. 4:8a)

Listening to God and your ability to hear his voice will grow with practice. At the beginning of your journey of listening to God, there will be moments when God speaks to you that you will know without a shadow of a doubt that it is God speaking. God does this on purpose to encourage you and help you tune in to the way that he speaks. In these obvious God speaking moments you do not need to use any of your faith to believe that it is God. But, you will find that there will be times in listening to God that it is more difficult to tell immediately if God is speaking. The difference between your voice and God's voice can be subtle. The subtle voice of God requires you to choose faith and boldness to speak out or act on what you are sensing. Sometimes the only way to know if it is God's voice that you are hearing is by acting on what he says or by speaking it out.

"The Lord said, "Go out and stand on the mountain in the presence of the Lord, for the Lord is about to pass by." Then a great and powerful wind tore the mountains apart and shattered the rocks before the Lord, but the Lord was not in the wind. After the wind there was an earthquake, but the Lord was not in the earthquake. After the earthquake came a fire, but the Lord was not in the fire. And after the fire came a gentle whisper." (1 Kings 19:11-12 NIV)

Growing in hearing God's voice is paying attention to subtleties; God's gentle whisper. Many people assume that as their listening matures that the subtlety of God's voice will disappear. This may not happen. You will likely continue to have times when God's voice is loud, and then times when it was still and small. As you continue to press into God, he will continue to come close to you.

Growth Patterns for Hearing God's Voice:

Growing and maturing in hearing God's voice can follow a typical growth pattern:

Engaging Faith and Desire increases Your Ability to hear God's Voice:

As you continue to desire to hear God's voice, he will speak to you in different ways and your sensitivity to his voice will improve. Your faith and desire play a key role in continuing to grow in hearing God's voice. Often when God begins to speak to you in a new way that you are not familiar with, his voice will sound loud and obvious. With time you will become familiar with the new way that he is speaking to you. This is usually when his voice becomes more subtle, and sounds more like your voice. Remember at this point that his voice is becoming more and more at home in your heart. Do not engage with thoughts of doubt.

God's subtle voice is just as valid as his obvious or loud voice. Continue to engage your faith that he wants to speak to you and engage your desire to draw close to him in relationship. A helpful tip to remember is how it felt when he first began speaking in this new way. When his voice becomes more familiar it will feel similar, just more subtle.

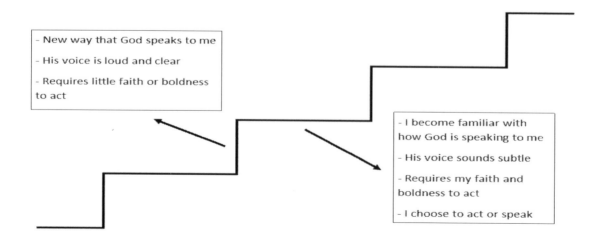

Engaging Doubt Stifles Your Ability to Hear God's Voice:

The truth of the following scriptures are for <u>you</u>. These verses emphasize relationship and communication between yourself and God, Jesus and Holy Spirit.

"That is what the Scriptures mean when they say, 'No eye has seen, no ear has heard, and no mind has imagined what God has prepared for those who love him.' But it was to us that God revealed these things by his Spirit. For his Spirit searches out everything and shows us God's deep secrets." (1 Cor. 2:9-10)

"My sheep listen to my voice; I know them, and they follow me." (Jn. 10:27)

"I no longer call you slaves, because a master doesn't confide in his slaves. Now you are my friends, since I have told you everything the Father told me." (Jn. 15:15)

Doubt is a tactic of Satan to try keep you from continuing to hear God's voice and deepening your relationship with God. He will try to sow thoughts of doubt to have you believe that you can't hear God's voice, or that God doesn't want to speak to you, or that you are going to do it wrong. The truth is that as a child of God you hear his voice and that he calls you friend. Friendship involves two way communication.

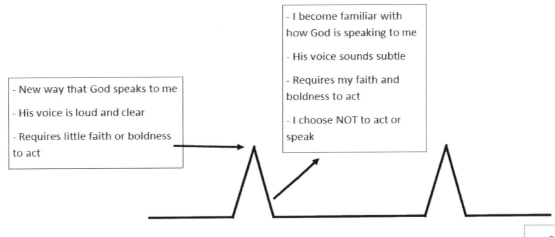

If you only speak or act when God's voice is loud and clear, and you know for sure that it is God, you will miss all of the subtle times that he speaks. Learn how to hear the gentle whisper of God.

God knows the best way for you to receive information from him. How you hear from the Lord and your listening to God may grow in a different way than described. Trust God's way for you; he can individualize your growth pattern.

Whatever your listening to God journey looks like, there is a part that you actively play. Learning to hear God's voice is like an art; listening improves and is refined with practice. The following are some tips that may help you in fine tuning and practicing listening:

Tips to Continue to Grow in Hearing God's Voice:

1. Find at least one dominant way that God speaks to you.

Everyone has at least one way that they hear/sense/perceive God's voice. Learning to hear God's voice is like tuning into a favorite radio station on a radio: you listen for the announcer that you know and the songs that they play. Like the familiar radio station, Father God, Jesus, Holy Spirit and the Bible are familiar to you. Listen for their voice and the essence of who they are. When you are able to target one way that God speaks to you, you can then actively engage God through this avenue.

Many times people become so accustomed to how God speaks personally to them, they have thought it was their own voice. Biblical community is valuable in helping others see how they are hearing from God. When someone in Deeper speaks to you and you feel the truth of God speaking through them, tell them! This will help them target how God personally speaks.

_____

_____

_____

_____

_____

_____

_____

_____

_____

2. Learn how others in your group hear from God.

As your Deeper group practices listening to God, pay attention to how others receive their information from God. As you learn the variety of ways that God speaks to his people, it will increase your awareness of the possibilities of how he may want to speak to you. Sometimes all God needs is an openness to begin communicating in a different way. Engage with God in how you know to listen to him, and desire other ways for him to speak to you.

_____

_____

_____

_____

_____

3. Journal what you are hearing/sensing/perceiving from God.

Write down what you sense the Lord saying to you. Journaling captures the details. Remember that sometimes when you are listening, it may not be clear in the moment if it is God speaking or if it is yourself. Time will sometimes grow the fruit when it is God's voice, and journaling makes it easier to re-visit past listening times.

_____

_____

_____

_____

_____

4. Act when you sense the Lord is asking you to do or say something.

Taking action is sometimes the only way that you know if it is from God or not. Be willing to act and take risks. This sometimes requires faith and boldness; this is a choice! Be faithful to steward what the Lord is giving you.

_____

_____

_____

_____

_____

_____

_____

_____

5. Look for supernatural fruit as evidence that God has spoken to you.

As you are hearing God's voice and then following the principles of Deeper (lining up what you hear with the Bible and God's character), then you should be left with words that will encourage you, edify you and comfort you. At the very least you have encouraged yourself in 100% of your power. If it was your voice that you heard, then you have done exactly what the Bible asks us to do: "Encourage one another and build each other up." (1 Thess. 5:11) You just happen to be the 'one another'!

You may be wondering if the words you heard were from yourself or from God. If this is the case, look for the fruit. We have all felt the fruit of human encouragement: you are uplifted, inspired, and motivated. If the words you heard were from God, however, you will experience supernatural fruit in the words:

- Truth and life (Jesus is called truth and life. – Jn. 14:6)
- Love (God is love. – 1 Jn. 4:8)
- Freedom (Spirit of God releases freedom. – 2 Cor. 3:17)
- Joy, peace, kindness, goodness, gentleness (fruit of Holy Spirit. – Gal. 5:22-23)
- Wisdom that is: pure, peace loving, gentle, willing to yield, full of mercy (Jas. 3:17)
- You are spiritually and positively changed in the interaction (2 Cor. 3:18)
- You are shown things that there is no way that you could know except through divine revelation (God conceals things, and I have the privilege to discover them. – Prov. 25:2)

Supernatural fruit comes from God, Jesus and Holy Spirit and impacts you at a level that human words cannot. Sometimes you will feel the supernatural fruit even as the words are spoken out, but sometimes the fruit grows with time.   If any of this fruit is evident in the words that you are hearing, then this is God speaking to you! You are on the right path! Keep pressing on in your relationship with God and your listening in faith!

_____

_____

_____

_____

_____

If hearing God's voice is not coming easily for you, keep practicing. Don't become discouraged! Remember that the Bible is the primary way that God speaks to his children. Even if the Bible is the only way that God speaks to you, that is enough!

Listening Exercise

A Place to 'Come Away'

Just as Jesus would regularly leave the crowd and his disciples to spend time with his Father, and so should we make this a rhythm in our life. Our listening exercise today will help you in meeting with a member of the Trinity in a special place of their choosing. Either listen in the way that you have found that is the most natural, or begin this exercise by engaging in vision through your imagination.

Prepare yourself to abide in Jesus.

Pray the following prayer to prepare yourself to hear God's voice:

"In the name of Jesus, I silence the voice of any spirits that are contrary to Holy Spirit. I joyfully submit my spirit, soul, imagination, and body to you, Holy Spirit. I welcome you Holy Spirit to speak to me, I declare that I am God's child and I hear his voice."

As you ask God, Jesus or Holy Spirit the following questions, engage your faith and trust that the first thing that you see, hear, sense is from God, and then ask more questions. Remember, when you are done listening, to line up what you received with the Bible and the character of God.

Ask the following questions:

"Which member of the Trinity is going to meet with me?"

_____

"Where is a secret place (real or imaginary) for us to meet?"

_____

_____

_____

_____

_____

_____

_____

"Why did you pick this place?"

_____

_____

_____

_____

_____

_____

_____

"What do you want to say to me here in this place you have chosen for us?"

_____

_____

_____

_____

_____

_____

_____

_____

_____

_____

NOTE: If you are having difficulty engaging with a place, picture with your imagination the cross of Jesus and use this as a starting place for Holy Spirit to add to.

Now that you have a meeting place with Father God, Jesus, or Holy Spirit, you can go back here at any time to commune with them, talk to them, etc. This is your special meeting place – come away often!

Going Deeper–Extra Practice
Come Away

Engage with Father, Jesus or Holy Spirit again and go back to your meeting place. Engage with the different members of the Trinity here. What else do they want to show you or speak to you? Ask them questions about yourself in this place.

Here are some ideas:

- What do you love about me? Why?
- What is something about me that makes you smile? Why?
- Where do you see that I am strong?
- Where do you see that I am weak?
- You promise that in my weakness you are strong. What is a strong part of you that you want to give me to cover my weakness?

Deeper - Part One

ENCOUNTER SESSION 6
Stewarding Truth

"(JESUS) GAVE ME BEAUTY FOR ASHES, THE OIL OF JOY FOR MOURNING, THE GARMENT OF PRAISE FOR THE SPIRIT OF HEAVINESS." ISAIAH 61:3 (NKJV)

JESUS HAD BEEN SPEAKING THIS VERSE TO ME FROM ISAIAH. I WAS COMING OUT OF A DIFFICULT SEASON, AND I COULD HEAR JESUS BECKONING ME TO COME TO HIM. I WAS SO USED TO COMING TO JESUS WITH PASSION AND EXUBERANT WORSHIP, TO COME TO JESUS WITH ASHES, MOURNING AND HEAVINESS SEEMED LIKE SUCH A PATHETIC OFFERING. I HESITATED. HE TOLD ME THAT AS I GIVE MY ASHES TO HIM, HE PROMISES ME BEAUTY, OIL OF JOY, AND A GARMENT OF PRAISE. WHAT HAPPENS IS A SUPERNATURAL EXCHANGE. JESUS ONLY ASKS ME TO COME AND OFFER TO HIM WHAT I HAVE. MY OFFERING IS SUPERNATURALLY TRANSFORMED INTO SOMETHING BEAUTIFUL.

WWW.DEANNASDECORATIVEDESIGNS.CA

ORIGINAL ACRYLIC PAINTINGS AND PRINTS BY
DEANNA OELKE

Worship Reflections

Journal, Draw, Doodle

Deeper—Encounter Session 6

Stewarding Truth

Embrace the sanctification process

As you are listening to Holy Spirit, the spoken words of truth may just be the beginning of the journey that Holy Spirit has for you. Journeying with Holy Spirit into deeper relationship with Father and Jesus is not just about listening. There is a parallel work of sanctification, healing and restoration that he desires to accomplish. Holy Spirit speaks words of life, love, truth and freedom. But, often these words are confronting the work of Satan: fear, lies, bondage and death.

When you hear words of living truth from Holy Spirit, you may have an emotional response - you may cry, feel like you could cry or have another strong feeling. Emotional responses are common when truth and words of life are spoken. You may not even understand why you are having an emotional response. Sometimes there is a work that Holy Spirit is doing at a spirit level that has not yet been brought to your mind and understanding.

Pay attention to how you respond to Holy Spirit's truth that he directly speaks to you or that you receive from others through prophetic words. Do you feel relief, healing?

Sometimes Holy Spirit's truth is ending a work that he is doing in your life, but sometimes his spoken truth is just the beginning of the work that he wants to do. It is important to know how to steward truth and allow Holy Spirit to do the work that he desires.

When you have a response to truth, begin to engage with Holy Spirit:

Is there anything else that you want to say to me?

Is this truth a finishing work, or the beginning of a new work you want to do?

Do you simply want me to feel my feelings in your presence, and posture myself to receive from you?

Sometimes all that Holy Spirit is asking is for us to submit, rest and receive from him. If you sense that Holy Spirit wants to do a work at a spirit level, posture yourself in the same way that you would if you were engaging in soaking (like you did during worship). Play worship music quietly in the background if you like. Position yourself to abide in Jesus (saying 'yes' with your spirit, soul and body) and allow Holy Spirit to do a work within you. He may give you understanding as to what he is doing/healing/restoring, or he may desire that you simply trust him with the process.

_____

_____

_____

_____

_____

_____

_____

_____

_____

Is there a wound that needs to be healed?

Pain is a common response to something within that needs healing. We each have a choice as to how to respond to pain:

- Ignore it and push it aside. Please realize that if this is your response and Holy Spirit desires to bring healing, it will come up again in the future.
- Take your pain to Jesus. Choose to trust him. Ask Jesus to lead you into healing and wholeness. He knows the perfect process for you to receive healing from the Great Physician.

Is there a character issue within me that you want to deal with?

The Lord disciplines those he loves (Heb. 12:6). Be quick to submit and say 'yes' to the work that Holy Spirit wants to do, and then do your part in cooperating with him. When God is working on a character issue in our lives, it involves submission to Jesus, discipline and good choices on our part.

As your ability to hear God's voice grows, desire holiness. Holy Spirit will be quick to honor this desire, as this is his heart for you.

Is there a lie I believed from Satan that needs to be replaced by truth?

This will be the focus of our teaching in Deeper this week.

Whatever Holy Spirit wants to do, ensure that you allow him to complete the work that he has started. Remember, there is no condemnation for those who are in Christ Jesus. As lies, character issues, wounds, etc. bubble to the surface, be quick to run to Jesus for his sanctifying work to be accomplished in your life. You are never disqualified from being God's child; he will always love you. He knows all of the issues that are in your life that need to be dealt with. Trust Holy Spirit and his timing in bringing issues to your attention. His timing is perfect for you.

_____

_____

_____

_____

_____

_____

_____

_____

_____

_____

_____

My Identity

Often truth that Holy Spirit speaks to us is related to and impacts our identity. Your identity is formed by your views and your beliefs about:

- Your relationship with the Holy Trinity.
- Who you are in Jesus Christ.
- Who you are created to be.

My Relationship with the Trinity
Truth: I am a son/daughter of God

"For you are all children of God through faith in Christ Jesus." (Gal. 3:26)

"And you must love the Lord your God with all your heart, all your soul, and all your strength." (Deut. 6:5)

Our first and greatest commandment: Love the Lord your God with all your heart, soul and strength is about relationship with Father God, Jesus and Holy Spirit. As you journey deeper with the Holy Trinity, Satan will try to slow your journey, interfere with your relationships, and try to sow lies about Father God, Jesus and Holy Spirit. Satan is called the father of lies (Jn. 8:44). Lying is one of his strategies. Often lies are attached to wounding, experiences, or our feelings. Hurtful experiences can make lies easier to believe.

_____

_____

_____

_____

Who I Am in Jesus Christ
Truth: I am a new person in Jesus Christ

"This means that anyone who belongs to Christ has become a new person. The old life is gone; a new life has begun!" (2 Cor. 5:17)

"What counts is whether we have been transformed into a new creation. May God's peace and mercy be upon all who live by this principle; they are the new people of God." (Gal. 6:15b-16)

At times the words that Holy Spirit speaks to us are rooted in this foundational truth: I am a new person in Jesus Christ. Satan wants to keep us from fully knowing who we are in Jesus, or he wants us to relate to our old, dead nature. Satan lies to us about who we are to keep us from living as a new person in the power of Jesus Christ. Our identity and who we are in Jesus Christ is vitally important to living in the fullness and the freedom of Christianity. Our Going Deeper: Extra Practice will focus on meditating on scripture and declarations of our identity in Jesus.

_____

_____

_____

_____

_____

_____

_____

_____

_____

Being Who I was Created to Be
Truth: I am fearfully and wonderfully made

"I praise you because I am fearfully and wonderfully made; your works are wonderful, I know that full well." (Ps. 139:14 NIV)

As you engage in relationship with God and live in who you are in Jesus Christ, you will discover who you were created to be - unique and wonderful! Holy Spirit will show you details about yourself that he loves. As you learn about yourself, and embrace who God created you to be, you will develop a healthy, godly self-love, and praise God for the way that he made you! You can then live in the fullness of your gifting, personality and uniqueness.

Satan would want you to believe that loving the way God made you will foster pride. This belief will cause you to shrink back from fully embracing who you were created to be. If you are concerned about falling into pride, ask Holy Spirit to show you when you have a prideful attitude. He will honour this prayer, and show you how to adjust.

Using truth to replace lies:

When you have a response to truth that Holy Spirit has spoken to you, and you realize you have believed a lie that is contrary to truth of the Bible, you can step into freedom from this lie in the following way. Remember that God knows what you are thinking, but Satan does not. When you are stepping out of a hold that Satan has had on you (like believing a lie) make sure you speak out loud. Let Satan hear that he is losing the power of the lie over you.

How to break the hold of a lie:

- What is the lie that you have believed?

  - Ex: Lie I believed: "I have to perfect before I can come to God."

- Repent out loud for believing this lie.

  - Ex: "Jesus forgive me for believing that I have to have my life together and be perfect before I can come to you or God."

- Replace the lie with truth. This may be truth revealed by Holy Spirit, or it simply may be finding a scripture that combats the lie that you have believed. Declare out loud who you are in Jesus Christ.

  - Ex: "Thank you, Jesus, that as a new person in you, I can have the boldness, courage and confidence of free access to Father God. I can approach God with freedom and without fear. I am righteous and holy." (Eph. 4:24)

- Declare out loud: "In the name of Jesus, I silence the voice of the enemy in speaking the lie that I have to be perfect before I can come to God. The Bible says that I can approach God with freedom and confidence."

Fighting With Truth

When a lie has been replaced with truth, use it as the sword of the Spirit; fight with it! Receiving truth to replace lies is just the start of walking into victory. You now need to live in the truth. Do not allow Satan to steal this truth from you. As you walk in truth, you will be walking in new victory.

Strategies:

- Write out the truth and corresponding Bible verses that were given to you by Jesus, Holy Spirit or Father God. Put them somewhere that you will see them on a regular basis.
- Memorize the Bible verses.
- Meditate on the Bible verses.
- Declare the truth out loud. You need to hear it, and Satan needs to be reminded of what you are believing. Declaring the Word of God out loud is spiritual warfare.
- Take every thought captive to the obedience of Christ (2 Cor. 10:4, 5). As thoughts come into your mind, ensure that they are lining up the thoughts with the truth of God's Word. If thoughts are not lining up with truth, these may be lies that Satan is trying to have you own for yourself and then believe. If this happens, speak out loud: "No, this is a lie. Be quiet in the name of Jesus", and then speak truth out loud.
- As you are learning to live with new truth, Holy Spirit may show you behaviours that need to change. Trust his timing and his ways. Be quick to change as he shows you.

Are there other ways that you or others in your group have used truth or Bible verses to fight with?

_____

_____

_____

_____

_____

_____

As you journey deeper with the Holy Trinity, you will continue to spiritually grow and change. Sometimes growth and changes are exciting, and sometimes they are painful. In those times when you are tempted to shrink back from the pain, ask yourself, "Do I trust Jesus?". God desires you to live in the fullness of who he created you to be. Jesus desires you to live in the fullness of who you are in him. And, Holy Spirit is willing to journey with you and empower you! Christianity is such an amazing opportunity to have such beautiful relationships with the Trinity and all the while discover who we truly are in Jesus: healed, whole, delivered and free!

"I pray that from his glorious, unlimited resources he will empower you with inner strength through his Spirit. Then Christ will make his home in your hearts as you trust in him. Your roots will grow down into God's love and keep you strong. And may you have the power to understand, as all God's people should, how wide, how long, how high, and how deep his love is." (Eph. 3:16-18)

Listening Exercise

Targeting Lies

The following listening exercise will help you in targeting lies that you have believed specifically in your relationship with Father God, Jesus, and Holy Spirit. This exercise will also allow for any inner healing that needs to occur.

Pray to prepare yourself to hear God's voice. Remember to write down the first impression or thought that you have as you are listening. When you are done listening, then go back and ensure that what you have written lines up with the Bible and God's character.

Think about Jesus in a spiritual way.

Ask Jesus if there is a lie that you have believed about him.

_____

_____

_____

_____

_____

_____

_____

_____

_____

_____

Ask Jesus to show you when you first believed this lie.

_____

_____

_____

_____

_____

_____

If a situation is brought to mind, forgive people as necessary. Repent if there is any way that you sinned in this situation.

_____

_____

_____

_____

_____

_____

Repent for believing the lie and renounce the lie.

Ask Jesus for truth related to this situation, and a truth statement to specifically combat the lie you have believed.

_____

_____

_____

_____

_____

Ask Jesus if there is anything else that he would want to say to you.

_____

_____

_____

_____

_____

Think about Holy Spirit in a spiritual way.

Ask Holy Spirit if there is a lie that you have believed about him.

_____

_____

_____

_____

_____

Ask Holy Spirit to show you when you first believed this lie.

_____

_____

_____

_____

_____

If a situation is brought to mind, forgive people as necessary. Repent if there is any way that you sinned in this situation.

_____

_____

_____

_____

_____

_____

Repent for believing the lie and renounce the lie.

Ask Holy Spirit for truth related to this situation, and a truth statement to specifically combat the lie you have believed.

_____

_____

_____

_____

_____

Ask Holy Spirit if there is anything else that he would want to say to you.

_____

_____

_____

Think about Father God in a spiritual way.

Ask Father if there is a lie that you have believed about him.

_____

_____

_____

_____

_____

Ask Father to show you when you first believed this lie.

_____

_____

_____

_____

If a situation is brought to mind, forgive people as necessary. Repent if there is any way that you sinned in this situation.

_____

_____

_____

_____

_____

Repent for believing the lie and renounce the lie.

Ask Father for truth related to this situation, and a truth statement to specifically combat the lie you have believed.

_____

_____

_____

Ask Father if there is anything else that he would want to say to you.

_____

_____

_____

_____

_____

_____

_____

_____

_____

_____

_____

_____

<u>Going Deeper–Extra Practice</u>

The following are truth statements. Meditate on these statements and the Bible verses. Ask Holy Spirit which statements that he would like to highlight to you. Ask him questions, and journey with him.

Who I am in Jesus Christ:

As a disciple, I am a friend of Jesus Christ. Jn. 15:15

I have been given the mind of Christ. 1 Cor. 2:16

I am free forever from condemnation. Rom. 8:1

I may approach God with freedom and confidence. Eph. 3:12

I have been raised up and seated with Christ in heaven. Eph. 2:6

I am an alien and stranger to this world I temporarily live in. 1 Pet. 2:11

I am hidden with Christ in God. Col. 3:1-4

I am chosen of God, holy, and dearly loved. Col. 3:12

I am righteous and holy. Eph. 4:24

I am God's child. Jn. 1:12

I have been redeemed and forgiven of all my sins. Col. 1:13-14

I am free from any condemnation brought against me & I cannot be separated from the love of God. Rom. 8:31-39

I have been given the Holy Spirit as a pledge guaranteeing my inheritance to come. Eph. 1:13-14

I am a citizen of heaven. Phil. 3:20

I have not been given a spirit of fear but of power, love and a sound mind. 2 Tim. 1:7

I have been justified (completely forgiven and made righteous). Rom. 5:1

I have been chosen by God and adopted as His child. Eph. 1:3-8

I am a member of Christ's body. 1 Cor. 12:27

I am a son/daughter of light and not of darkness. 1Thess. 5:5

I am united with the Lord, and I am one with him in spirit. 1 Cor. 6:17

I have been bought with a price and I belong to God. 1 Cor. 6:19-20

I am complete in Christ. Col. 2:9-10

I am God's workmanship. Eph. 2:10

I am born of God and the evil one cannot touch me. 1 Jn. 5:18

I am assured that God works for my good in all circumstances. Rom. 8:28

I have been crucified with Christ and it is no longer I who live, but Christ lives in me. Gal 2:20

I have direct access to the throne of grace through Jesus Christ. Heb. 4:14-16

I can do all things through Christ, who strengthens me. Phil. 4:13

I am a chosen race, a royal priesthood, a holy nation, a people for God's own possession to proclaim the excellences of him. 1 Pet. 2:9-10

I am not the great "I Am", but by the grace of God I am what I am. Ex. 3:14; Jn. 8:24, 25, 28; 1 Cor. 15:10

Deeper - Part One

ENCOUNTER SESSION 7
Dreams

"MAY YOU HAVE THE POWER TO UNDERSTAND, AS ALL GOD'S PEOPLE SHOULD, HOW WIDE, HOW LONG, HOW HIGH, AND HOW DEEP HIS LOVE IS. MAY YOU EXPERIENCE THE LOVE OF CHRIST, THROUGH IT IS TOO GREAT TO UNDERSTAND FULLY. THEN YOU WILL BE MADE COMPLETE WITH ALL THE FULLNESS OF LIFE AND POWER THAT COMES FROM GOD."
EPHESIANS 3:18-19

HORSES TO ME REPRESENT POWER AND AUTHORITY. WHEN I FINISHED PAINTING THIS HORSE, HIS BODY AND HIS EYES LOOKED SO GENTLE TO ME. I DID NOT UNDERSTAND HOW THE CONCEPT OF POWER AND AUTHORITY COULD HAVE THE ESSENCE OF GENTLENESS. WHEN I CAME ACROSS THIS PASSAGE FROM EPHESIANS, THEN I UNDERSTOOD. NO ONE CAN STAND AGAINST GOD'S POWER AND AUTHORITY, YET HE IS LOVE. HIS LOVE CARRIES THE ESSENCE OF WHO HE IS: GENTLE.

WWW.DEANNASDECORATIVEDESIGNS.CA
ORIGINAL ACRYLIC PAINTINGS AND PRINTS BY
DEANNA OELKE

Power, Authority, and Love

Worship Reflections

Journal, Draw, Doodle

Deeper—Encounter Session 7

Dreams

"For God may speak in one way, or in another, yet man does not perceive it. In a dream in a vision of the night, when deep sleep falls upon men, while slumbering on their beds, then he opens the ears of men, and seals their instruction." (Job 33:14-16 NKJV)

"And afterward, I will pour out my Spirit on all people. Your sons and daughters will prophesy, your old men will dream dreams, your young men will see visions." (Joel 2:28 NIV)

Dreams in the Bible

Dreams in the Bible were considered a legitimate way that God speaks.

The following are some of the people that God spoke to through dreams in the Bible.

- Jacob (Gen. 28:12, 31:10)
- Laban (Gen. 31:24)
- Joseph (Gen. 37:5,9)
- The butler and the baker (Gen. 40:5)
- Pharaoh (Gen. 41:1, 5)
- The man in Gideon's army (Jud. 7:13)
- Solomon (1 Kings 3:5)
- Nebuchadnezzar (Dan. 2:3, 4:5)
- Daniel (Dan. 7:1)

- Joseph (Matt. 1:20, 2:13, 19, 22)
- The wise men (Matt. 2:12)
- Pilate's wife (Matt. 27:19)
- Others: _____
- _____
- _____
- _____
- _____

There are only two known dream interpreters in the Bible:

- Joseph
- Daniel

Joseph and Daniel both stated that their ability to interpret dreams came from God. Their God given ability far surpassed the ability of the other dream interpreters that were not children of God. This is an important truth for us to remember as we take a biblical view of dream interpretation. Relying on God is key; he is the source for correct interpretation.

Dream interpretation has been dropped by the Western church and has been picked up by the New Age and the world. The New Age and the world do not have Holy Spirit to rely on for leading into the kingdom of God in the interpretive process. They are relying on interpretive models and symbolism that is soul led. It is time that Christians take back the art of dream interpretation as we rely on Holy Spirit to lead us into truth for interpreting dreams.

Before we go through a simple dream interpretation process, it is important to note that not all dreams are from God. Just like in your listening (we can hear from ourselves, God and Satan), we can also have dreams from ourselves, God and Satan.

As you begin to dream, pay attention to your dreams. Rely on Holy Spirit to help you sift through your dreams to discover the ones that are from God.

A Simple Interpretative Process

Without God's help, we will not be able to understand dreams; it is more than just having the necessary tools to interpret dreams. Just because you are prophetic, does not mean you will necessarily be good at dream interpretation. Some people are better at dream interpretation than others. A great way to see if you have the ability to interpret dreams is to practice. Practice on yourself with your dreams and with others using their dreams.

As you are interpreting your dreams:

- Rely on Holy Spirit as your main source and guide.
- Become familiar with some dream symbols or look up dream symbols
- Ask Holy Spirit the meaning.
- Talk to prophetic friends and gain their help in interpreting your dreams.

Once you become more familiar with dream symbols, try to avoid a 'plug and play' interpretation. Symbols can be used by God in both dreams and visions. However, dreams tend to be more symbolic in nature, while visions are more literal. The use of symbols is only a guide. Your ultimate symbol guide and interpreter is Holy Spirit.

Simple Dream Interpretation Steps:

1. Dreams that we have can come from 3 sources: God, ourselves and Satan. Do you immediately have a sense if the dream is from God, from yourself or from Satan?

_____

_____

2. Begin to record dreams that you sense are significant and you sense may be from God, even if you don't understand them or are able to interpret them initially.

_____

_____

3. If you sense the dream is from Satan, ask God what he would want to speak into the dream. Imagine the dream again, and ask Jesus to walk with you through the dream. Watch what Jesus is doing and ask Jesus what he wants to speak to you at key points of the dream. Flip the dream as you walk through it with Jesus according to the truth of his Word.

   - Ex: if you have a dream about your life involving destruction and turmoil, walk through the dream with Jesus in the truth of Jeremiah 29:11. Flip the dream and re-imagine the destruction and turmoil being overcome by God's plans that will prosper, not harm you, plans that will give you hope and a future.
   - If you have frequent nightmares, begin to pray God's covering or pray the blood of Jesus to cover you and your dreams before you go to sleep.

_____

_____

4. If you think the dream might be from God, think through the following:

    - Try to reduce the dream to its simplest form. If you could title the dream, what would you title it?
    - Determine the focus of the dream. Ask: "Who is this dream about? Who, or what, is the center of attention?"
    - What were your feelings in the dream? Are they positive, negative, neutral?
    - What are some important symbols in the dream? Pay particular attention to the following:

        - Colours
        - Numbers
        - Names of people
            - Does the name represent an actual person such as someone you know? If yes, what does this person mean to you? What might this person represent?
            - Or, the person might not be the focus, it might be their name and the meaning of their name. Look up the meaning of the name on baby name websites.

_____

_____

_____

5. Look up the meaning of the main symbols of the dream. **tehillahdreams.com** is an excellent website which uses a variety of good Christian resources for its dream symbols. This website also has a dream symbol search engine.

_____

_____

6. Rely on Holy Spirit to sense for an accurate interpretation. Steward your dream interpretation in the same way you would in listening to the voice of God: line up your interpretation with the Bible and the character of God. Once you sense from Holy Spirit that you have an accurate dream interpretation, discern what your part is. Is there something that God wants you to do? Is God requiring action on your part? Continue to press in to Holy Spirit to find out what is next. If you sense that you don't have an accurate interpretation, lay the dream aside and come back to it when the Holy Spirit leads you.

_____

_____

_____

_____

_____

_____

_____

This whole dream interpretation process may take minutes, weeks, months or sometimes years. Trust Holy Spirit and his leading you into the dream interpretation and the stewardship of the interpretation.

(If you are interested in learning more about dreams and Christian dream interpretation, Streams Ministry would be an excellent place to start. Streams Ministry is a prophetic ministry of John Paul Jackson. Many prophetic leaders of today have been trained in dream interpretation by John Paul. He offers courses on-line as well as dream cards that are quick reference cards for searching the meaning of colours, numbers, common dream symbols, and top 20 dreams.)

<u>Listening Exercise</u>

Dream Interpretation

Write down significant points that others spoke to you related to your dream.

_____

_____

_____

_____

_____

_____

_____

_____

_____

_____

_____

_____

_____

Going Deeper–Extra Practice
Dream Interpretation

Continue to practice dream interpretation on your own dreams and other's dreams. This is often an easy open door to initiate conversation with non-prophetic Christians and non-Christians since most people dream. You can approach dream interpretation with others in the following way: "I have recently learned dream interpretation, and I was wondering if you would let me practice on you? Do you have a dream that I could try to interpret?" After walking through the dream interpretation process, ask them if they feel that this is accurate. Also, don't be afraid to say you don't know if you receive no interpretation from Holy Spirit.

Deeper - Part Two

"THEN, AFTER DOING ALL THOSE THINGS, I WILL POUR OUT MY SPIRIT UPON ALL PEOPLE. YOUR SONS AND DAUGHTERS WILL PROPHESY. YOUR OLD MEN WILL DREAM DREAMS, AND YOUR YOUNG MEN WILL SEE VISIONS." JOEL **2:28**

I WAS PRAYING ONE NIGHT WHEN INSTANTLY I SAW A VISION OF FATHER GOD HOLDING A CLAY POT. AS HE TIPPED THE POT I SAW WATER POURING OUT. THE END OF THE WATER TURNED INTO A HEARD OF GALLOPING HORSES. BEFORE I EVEN HAD A CHANCE TO ASK HIM WHAT THIS MEANT, I HEARD HIM SAY, "IN THE LAST DAYS, I WILL POUR MY SPIRIT ON ALL FLESH". HOLY SPIRIT IS REPRESENTED BY THE HERD OF HORSES. THERE IS A SENSE OF INTENSITY, FOCUS AND INTENTIONALITY OF HOLY SPIRIT TO CARRY OUT THE WILL OF FATHER GOD.

WWW.DEANNASDECORATIVEDESIGNS.CA
ORIGINAL ACRYLIC PAINTINGS AND PRINTS BY
DEANNA OELKE

<u>Worship Reflections</u>

Journal, Draw, Doodle

Deanna's Reflections on Prophecy

Is it me, or is it God?

This is a common question when people are learning to hear God's voice. Hearing God's voice for yourself feels much safer and less risky than hearing God's voice for others and operating in the gift of prophecy. Sharing what you sense the Lord is saying with someone else requires more boldness on your part. Remember if you are staying within the guidelines of 1 Corinthians 14, and your prophetic words are comforting, encouraging and edifying, then at the very least you are encouraging the person with 100% of your own power. God thinks that encouraging each other in our own power is a good thing: "Encourage one another, and build each other up" (1 Thess. 5:11).

When you feel the witness of Holy Spirit and his gentle whisper, begin to act on it and speak out what you are sensing. Also, watch and listen to how people respond to you as you prophesy to them: Are they emotional as you speak? Do they affirm that this is exactly what they needed to hear? Do they affirm that God was speaking through you? As these responses happen, be affirmed that you are operating in the gift of prophecy.

Operating in the gift of prophecy is a balance between confidence in knowing you have the gift of prophecy and that you hear from God, and humility in knowing you are not perfect and that you will make mistakes.

The Battle Against Pride:

I believe one of the main ways that Satan tries to ensnare people with the gift of prophecy is through pride. As we operate in the gift of prophecy and sense and see things about people, we need to remember that even the gift of prophecy reveals only part of the whole picture (1 Cor. 13:9).

It can be very easy to slip into the attitude of: *"I know better than you because I hear from God"*. As God shows us things for people, we must be very careful to not judge them, especially when they make choices that are different than what we think is God's best. Remember that each Christian you prophesy over has Father God, Jesus and Holy Spirit to guide them in their lives. With non-Christians, trust God to draw them to himself, through his Spirit, his Word, and through believers. Our responsibility is to prophesy with love and then continue to love others in their journey, for without love in our gift of prophecy, we are nothing (1 Cor. 13:2).

Once others know that you have the gift of prophecy, they may come to you to hear from God. This is not necessarily a bad thing. When you become more familiar with your gift of prophecy, you will be able to access a prophetic word for anyone. Ask Holy Spirit how to respond to each individual when you are asked for a word. When you perceive that people are coming to you instead of listening to God for themselves, gently push them toward God and encourage them to hear God for themselves. In this way, you can help others from shortchanging themselves in their relationship with God and spur them on to develop greater intimacy with him.

When you do prophesy over others, ensure that all of your prophetic words push people into God. This can be easily done by saying, "Take what I have shared to Holy Spirit and ask him what he would want to add to what I have said to you. Ask Holy Spirit what else he would like to say to you". We want people to be dependent on God, not us.

Often people assume that when their prophetic gift matures, they will be 100% accurate in their prophetic words. I have found that this is not the case. Remember, we prophesy in part. I believe that God does this on purpose to keep us in a posture of humility in realizing that we can make mistakes. When we remain in love and stay within the guidelines of encouraging, comforting and edifying, even when we hear incorrectly, our prophetic words will still be an encouragement to the person receiving.

The gift of prophecy has a 'wow' factor to it. Often when people recognize that you have the gift of prophecy, they will be watching you. Often people will assume that the gift of prophecy means you are also a very spiritual person, with good character and a great relationship with God. The fact is a person can have a gift of prophecy but have flaws in their character. Holy Spirit gives the gift freely without the condition of spiritual maturity. Our desire as a prophetic people must be not only to speak the words of God, but also to live the Word of God. As you see your prophetic gift growing, I encourage you to pray this simple prayer: "God, don't let my prophetic gift outgrow my character."

Our experience in God affects how we speak prophetic words. If you find that you consistently receive negative words or have judgemental words versus mercy words, ask God why. Begin to journey with God and ask him what your view of him is. You will prophesy out of your view of God and your core values. If you live in the love of God, you will prophesy out of this love. The more you learn to receive love from Father God, the more you will communicate Father's love for others. 1 John 4:19 says, "We love because he first loved us." We have to learn to live in the fullness of God's love to be able to love others well.

Let us be a holy prophetic people whose hearts desire is to lift up and glorify the name of Jesus in all we say and do!

Deanna

...deep calls to deep...

Psalm 42:7

Deeper—Encounter Session 8

What is the Gift of Prophecy?

At this point in our Deeper journey, we will be shifting from a focus of listening to God for ourselves to listening to God for others. All of the same principles and ways that you have learned to listen to God for yourself will be applied to listening to God for others. This is the practice of the gift of prophecy. This gift from Holy Spirit truly does grow through practice. I encourage you to trust the voice of Holy Spirit that you have come to know over the past few weeks. I encourage you to be obedient and bold in speaking out what you sense the Holy Spirit saying to you for others. Faithfully steward what Holy Spirit is giving you, and he will continue to give you more for the edification of others.

As we operate in our gift of prophecy, it is important to know what the Bible says in the New Testament regarding the gift of prophecy. Let's focus on New Testament Bible verses to give ourselves a good biblical track for prophecy.

Holy Spirit Gives the Gift of Prophecy:

"A spiritual gift is given to each of us so we can help each other. To one person the Spirit gives the ability to give wise advice; to another the same Spirit gives a message of special knowledge. The same Spirit gives great faith to another, and to someone else the one Spirit gives the gift of healing. He gives one person the power to perform miracles, and another the ability to prophesy. He gives someone else the ability to discern whether a message is from the Spirit of God or from another spirit. Still another person is given the ability to speak in unknown languages, while another is given the ability to interpret what is being said. It is the one and only Spirit who distributes all these gifts. He alone decides which gift each person should have." (1 Cor. 12:7-11)

The gift of prophecy is one of the gifts given by Holy Spirit that is referenced in 1 Corinthians 12. This passage of scripture states that Holy Spirit decides which gift each person should have. You may receive the gift of prophecy from Holy Spirit simply by him releasing it to you and even without you asking for it. The posture on your part is one of openness and willingness for Holy Spirit to give to you what he chooses from this list of gifts in 1 Corinthians 12.

_____

_____

_____

_____

_____

_____

_____

Our Desire Releases Spiritual Gifts:

In 1 Corinthians 14 we read more specifically about the gift of prophecy. Within this passage are key principles:

We can receive the gift of prophecy by desire on our part.

"Let love be your highest goal! But you should also desire the special abilities the Spirit gives—especially the ability to prophesy." (1 Cor. 14:1)

Paul as a leader expresses his desire for the Corinthians.

"… I wish you could all prophesy." (I Cor. 14:5a)

Paul encourages the Corinthians to seek the gifts of Holy Spirit.

"Since you are so eager to have the special abilities the Spirit gives, seek those that will strengthen the whole church." (1 Cor. 14:12)

These verses capture the heart of Father God towards us so well. Even though 1 Corinthians 12 states that Holy Spirit alone decides who will receive his gifts, this passage in 1 Corinthians 14 says that desire on our part can release the gifts of Holy Spirit to us! Father wants us to desire the gifts of Holy Spirit; he wants to release the gift of prophecy to us! Sometimes he is simply waiting for us to express our desire for it.

_____

_____

_____

_____

_____

The Gift of Prophecy is For Encouragement:

The gift of prophecy strengthens, encourages, and comforts.

"One who prophesies strengthens others, encourages them, and comforts them." (1 Cor. 14:3)

Prophecy strengthens the entire church.

"...but one who speaks a word of prophecy strengthens the entire church. ...prophecy is greater than speaking in tongues ... so that the whole church will be strengthened." (1 Cor. 14:4, 5)

The gift of prophecy is not for our own edification; it is for the body of Christ. Do you desire to cooperate with Holy Spirit through the gift of prophecy to strengthen, encourage and comfort others in your biblical community? Then desire the gift of prophecy, and journey with Holy Spirit for him to release it to you!

Paul is clear here that prophecy is for: strengthening, encouraging and comforting other Christians. Prophecy is not to be used to point out sin, correct, or judge other believers. Within biblical community we will be correcting people, walking people through sin, and loving them in their issues. If someone needs to be corrected or confronted in your biblical community, ensure first that you are in relationship with the person, that you are following the prompting of Holy Spirit, and that it is done in love.

This <u>should not</u> be done with a spoken/prophetic word of God. You don't have to be prophetic to see the sin or the issues in people's lives. You have to be prophetic to find the treasures in people and in their hearts. Ask Holy Spirit to see the treasure; be a treasure hunter!

_____

_____

_____

Distinction Between the Logos Word and the Rhema Word of God:

Logos Word of God: "All Scripture is God-breathed and is useful for teaching, rebuking, correcting and training in righteousness, so that the servant of God may be thoroughly equipped for every good work." (2 Tim. 3:16-17 NIV)

Rhema Word of God: "The one who prophesies speaks to people for their strengthening, encouraging and comfort." (1 Cor. 14:3 NIV)

These two verses give a clear distinction between the role of the Logos and Rhema Word of God. The Logos (written Word of God) is for teaching, rebuking, correcting, and training in righteousness. The Rhema (spoken Word of God/prophetic word) is for strengthening, encouraging, and comforting. Sometimes Holy Spirit might show you things about a person that may be the reality of where they are, and this reality may not be encouraging. When this happens, ask Holy Spirit how he sees them. He will show you what they look like healed, whole, delivered in Jesus Christ. If you are unsure if your prophetic word is going to be strengthening, encouraging and comforting, ask yourself, "Would I want to receive this prophetic word for myself?" If not, ask Holy Spirit to help you adjust it into a strengthening, encouraging, and comforting word.

_____

_____

_____

_____

_____

_____

_____

Prophesying Requires us to Engage Faith:

"We have different gifts, according to the grace given to each of us. If your gift is prophesying, then prophesy in accordance with your faith." (Rom. 12:6 NIV)

Faith is confidence in what we hope for and assurance about what we do not see (Heb. 11:1). We can all choose to have faith, but also ask for the spiritual gift of supernatural faith as stated in 1 Corinthians 12:9. As we prepare to prophesy to someone, we need to engage faith and belief in the biblical principles of the gift of prophecy. We have faith that God desires to talk to his people. We also need to engage faith that Holy Spirit desires to cooperate with us to encourage, comfort and strengthen others. We can choose to have a little faith in this principle or a lot of faith; you then prophesy according to the level of faith you have.

Prophesy in Love:

"If I have the gift of prophecy and can fathom all mysteries and all knowledge, and if I have a faith that can move mountains, but do not have love, I am nothing." (1 Cor. 13:2 NIV)

We are <u>nothing</u> without love. This is a strong statement. Love should be our goal as we prophesy. As you are operating in your gift of prophecy, ask yourself: "As people see me using my prophetic gift, are they seeing and hearing the language of love?" The more you learn to love God, the better you will be able to love yourself and love others. You prophesy from what your relationship with Father God is like and what you know about his characteristics. The more we grow in our relationship with God and experience him as love, the better we will speak his language of love and release his nature of love.

We Prophesy in Part:

"Love never fails. But where there are prophecies, they will cease; where there are tongues, they will be stilled; where there is knowledge, it will pass away. For we know in part and we prophesy in part, but when completeness comes, what is in part disappears." (1 Cor. 13:8-10 NIV)

Do not assume that as God shows you details and gives insight about a person that you see the whole picture. We prophesy in part and see only part of the whole. Be faithful to deliver the 'part' that you see, and God will work in the person to show them the 'whole' in his timing and in his way.

God Values Order as We Prophesy:

"Let two or three people prophesy, and let the others evaluate what is said. But if someone is prophesying and another person receives a revelation from the Lord, the one who is speaking must stop. In this way, all who prophesy will have a turn to speak, one after the other, so that everyone will learn and be encouraged. Remember that people who prophesy are in control of their spirit and can take turns. For God is not a God of disorder but of peace, as in all the meetings of God's holy people. So, my dear brothers and sisters, be eager to prophesy, and don't forbid speaking in tongues. But be sure that everything is done properly and in order." (1 Cor. 14:29-33, 39-40)

This passage of scripture shows that prophesying in a group should be done in an orderly way, with everyone having a turn. You may feel an urgency at times in delivering a prophetic word. Remember that God is patient, and love is patient. Remember you are in control of your spirit, and you can take turns prophesying with others.

God Asks Us to Submit to Our Leaders:

"Obey your spiritual leaders, and do what they say. Their work is to watch over your souls, and they are accountable to God. Give them reason to do this with joy and not with sorrow. That would certainly not be for your benefit." (Heb. 13:17)

If you are giving prophetic words in a church, ensure that you are submitting to their leadership and are following their prophetic protocol. Operate in your gift of prophecy in a way that will be received by the people and your leadership. Be culturally relevant, and use words that will be accepted by the biblical community.

_____

_____

_____

_____

_____

_____

Listening Exercise

Using Your Prophetic Gift

Partner Prophesying:

In pairs, ask the Lord the following questions for each other. Share one at a time the revelations that you are receiving. Provide feedback to each other.

1. Jesus, what colour is this person like? Why? What does that mean?

   (Share with each other)

2. Ask God to give a Bible verse for the other person. Then ask him for one specific aspect/word/part of the verse that he is highlighting. Then ask him what he wants to tell the other person through it. (Avoid preaching the Word. Instead, hear the personal message that is on God's heart right now for your partner.)

   (Share)

3. Ask God to give you an inner picture/vision for your partner. Ask him what he wants to tell them through it.

   (Share)

4. Ask God to let you feel a certain emotion. Then ask God what it means for the other person; what exactly does he want to say through that?

   (Share)

Going Deeper–Extra Practice
Prophetic Practice

Try to integrate prophecy into your life outside of your Deeper community. Use any of the Deeper questions to help you receive something from Holy Spirit. As you interact with others, be aware of the people that you are prophesying over and adjust your words and present them in a way that they will be received. Try asking Holy Spirit questions for people you know, and for people you don't know. Try with people who are open to the prophetic, or new, or maybe do not yet know Jesus. If you know the person you are prophesying over, ask them to give you feedback.

Here are some ideas to help you listen to Holy Spirit for others:

- Ask Holy Spirit to help you write an encouraging note for someone.
- Ask Holy Spirit how he is praying for a friend/family member. Call them and ask if you can pray for them.
- As you are visiting with someone (over coffee, dinner, etc.), ask Holy Spirit what he loves about your friend. Tell them what Holy Spirit said.

If your word was accurate but was not received by the person, do not become discouraged. After your time together with the person, ask Holy Spirit how you could have done it differently. Learn from his suggestions. Realize that some people just don't want to receive prophetic words or don't know how to receive words. If they are resistant to your words, bless them and release them in their journey. If they are reluctant to receive the word because receiving a prophetic word is new to them, ask them if they want to learn more about the gift of prophecy, and simply teach them as the Holy Spirit leads you.

Ask Holy Spirit to bring people to you that are hungry for prophetic words of blessing, then practice your gift of prophecy. Bless others, and have fun!

Deeper - Part Two

ENCOUNTER SESSION 9
Differences Between Old and New Covenant Prophecy

Flaming Lion of Judah

I LOVE PAINTING JESUS AS THE LION OF JUDAH AND AS THE CONSUMING FIRE. I LOVE THE COMBINATION OF THE TWO NAMES. I HAVE PAINTED MANY VERSIONS OF JESUS IN THIS WAY. THIS TIME, I WANTED TO CAPTURE THE PROTECTIVE NATURE OF THE LORD OVER US AND HIS INTENTIONALITY TO FIGHT ON OUR BEHALF.

WWW.DEANNASDECORATIVEDESIGNS.CA
ORIGINAL ACRYLIC PAINTINGS AND PRINTS BY
DEANNA OELKE

Worship Reflections

Journal, Draw, Doodle

<u>Deeper—Encounter Session 9</u>

Differences Between Old and New Covenant Prophecy

Since the gift of prophecy is not commonly taught in churches, there is often a lack of understanding related to the gift of prophecy that comes from Holy Spirit. Often people think the gift of prophecy and New Testament prophets are the same as Old Testament prophecy and Old Testament prophets. There are significant differences between the two. These will be discussed to ensure that we are operating in the gift of prophecy within New Covenant principles and values. A significant shift happened in prophecy when Jesus died on the cross, fulfilling the law and the prophets, thus allowing us to step into New Covenant principles

Old and New Covenant:

<u>Old Covenant:</u>

"Indeed, there is no one on earth who is righteous, no one who does what is right and never sins." (Eccl. 7:20 NIV)

Old Testament prophets reminded people they could not perfectly follow the law and reminded them of their sin in falling short of God's standard. This led to prophets pointing to the people's desperate need for a saviour. The prophets pointed to Jesus and prophesied his coming.

Jesus fulfilled the Old Covenant:

"Do not think that I (Jesus) have come to abolish the Law or the Prophets; I have not come to abolish them but to fulfill them." (Matt. 5:17 NIV)

Jesus came to earth, fulfilled the law and the prophets and established a New Covenant. Where the first Adam failed and sinned, the last Adam (Jesus) fulfilled living a sinless life, died for us, was raised to life again and made a way for us to be reconciled to Father God.

New Covenant:

"Put on the new self, created to be like God in true righteousness and holiness." (Eph. 4:24 NIV)

In this New Covenant in Jesus Christ, our new self is righteous and holy! As New Covenant prophetic people we are to be aligned with the New Covenant values, not Old Covenant values. We are to point people to their new self, righteous and holy, not point them to their old sin nature.

_____

_____

_____

_____

_____

_____

_____

_____

Let's now focus on the differences between Old and New Covenant prophecy:

New Covenant prophecy embraces the ministry of reconciliation:

Old Covenant Prophecy	New Covenant Prophecy
Judged the people. (Ez. 18:30, Is. 1:4)	Encourages people and directs them back to God in the ministry of reconciliation. (1 Cor. 14:1-4, 2 Cor. 5:17-19)

"Judgement without mercy will be shown to anyone who has not been merciful. Mercy triumphs over judgement." (Jam. 2:13 NIV)

"Be merciful, just as your Father is merciful. Do not judge, and you will not be judged. Do not condemn, and you will not be condemned. Forgive, and you will be forgiven. Give, and it will be given to you. A good measure, pressed down, shaken together and running over, will be poured into your lap. For with the measure you use, it will be measured to you." (Luke 6:36-38 NIV)

As God's people, we release mercy to those who deserve judgement. We do not release judgement. This applies to us as we give prophetic words as well. We operate and release words of mercy instead of words of judgement.

"Therefore, if anyone is in Christ, the new creation has come: The old has gone, the new is here! All this is from God, who reconciled us to himself through Christ and gave us the ministry of reconciliation: that God was reconciling the world to himself in Christ, not counting people's sins against them. And he has committed to us the message of reconciliation." (2 Cor. 5:17-19 NIV)

In the New Covenant, we are given the ministry of reconciliation. Reconciliation is defined as changing for the better a relationship between two or more persons. We are challenged to draw people into a better relationship and friendship with Father God. This ministry of reconciliation is for all forms of ministry, including prophetic ministry. According to scripture, the ministry of reconciliation is, "not counting their trespasses against them". We will still sin, but in Jesus Christ our sins are not counted against us. As prophetic people our words should minister and restore the relationship between God and his people.

New Covenant prophecy calls us into our new identity and relationship with Jesus Christ:

Old Covenant Prophecy	New Covenant Prophecy
Points to sin calling for repentance and change of behavior. (Ez. 18:30)	Points to Jesus calling for repentance and change in relationship. (Luke. 5:32, Gal. 4:4-7)
Old Testament is a visitation culture where Holy Spirit visits people. (1 Sam. 10:10, Gen. 41:38, 1 Sam 16:13)	New Testament and New Covenant is a habitation culture where Holy Spirit inhabits people. (Jn. 14:16-18)

But when the set time had fully come, God sent his Son, born of a woman, born under the law, to redeem those under the law, that we might receive adoption to sonship. Because you are his sons, God sent the Spirit of his Son into our hearts, the Spirit who calls out, *"Abba*, Father." So you are no longer a slave, but God's child; and since you are his child, God has made you also an heir." (Gal. 4:4-7 NIV)

"And I will ask the Father, and he will give you another advocate to help you and be with you forever— the Spirit of truth. The world cannot accept him, because it neither sees him nor knows him. But you know him, for he lives with you and will be in you. I will not leave you as orphans; I will come to you." (Jn. 14:16-18 NIV)

"God's kindness is intended to lead us to repentance." (Rom. 2:4 NIV)

God's people before Jesus Christ did not have the working of the Holy Spirit within them. The Holy Spirit was given to select people in the Old Testament: kings, priests, prophets, and other select individuals.

Before Jesus Christ, the people were spiritually dead. They had the laws of God so that they could choose to obey God, but they could not follow the laws perfectly. Part of the role of the Old Testament prophet was to deliver a message from God to tell people when they were sinning and enact judgment for their sin. The Old Testament prophets were the voice of God to the people. Today, we too have the Bible to know how to obey and follow God, and we have Holy Spirit within us to be the voice of God in our lives and lead us to repentance.

Since the Old Testament prophets were speaking on behalf of God, and the people did not have the Spirit of God within them, the penalty for the prophets speaking an inaccurate prophetic word was death. Today, since we have Holy Spirit within us, anytime we hear a prophetic word spoken to us through another believer, we take this word to Holy Spirit to discern the accuracy and validity of the prophetic word.

Romans 2:4 says that God's kindness is intended to lead us to repentance. The Holy Spirit works out the sanctification process very uniquely for each person. As prophetic people, we call believers into New Covenant relationship with Father God, Jesus and Holy Spirit. We trust Jesus and Holy Spirit to lead people to see their sin; this is not our job with prophetic words.

_____

_____

_____

_____

_____

_____

Prophets:

Old Covenant Prophets & New Covenant Prophets

The label "prophet" is used to set individuals apart in ministry within the Old Testament and the New Testament.

- "Before I formed you in the womb I knew you, before you were born I set you apart; I appointed you as a prophet to the nations." (Jer. 1:5 NIV)

- "So Christ himself gave the apostles, the prophets, the evangelists, the pastors and teachers to equip his people for works of service…" (Eph. 4:11-12a NIV)

A common question that comes us with the discussion of the gift of prophecy and prophets is, 'Do prophets exist today?' Let's spend some time discussing New Covenant prophets according to this passage in Ephesians and how that relates to someone named a prophet today.

Prophets are not often in a prominent position within the North American church. For this reason, we will focus on some common questions related to New Testament prophets.

What is a New Testament prophet?

"Now these are the gifts Christ gave to the church: the apostles, the prophets, the evangelists, and the pastors and teachers. Their responsibility is to equip God's people to do his work and build up the church, the body of Christ." (Eph. 4:11-12)

The gift of prophecy is from Holy Spirit (1 Cor. 12), and we can access it by desire (1 Cor. 14:1). The prophet is a gift to the church from Jesus Christ. This is a call from Jesus Christ; this is not something that we can choose for ourselves. According to Ephesians 4, the prophet's responsibility is to equip God's people to do his work and build up the body of Christ.

Just because you have the gift of prophecy, does not mean that you are a prophet. The gift of prophecy and the call of a prophet are different and are separate from each other. Someone called to be a prophet by Jesus will have the gift of prophecy and will operate within the guidelines of New Covenant prophecy as previously discussed. Sometimes people who have named themselves a prophet believe that it is their right to deliver words of judgement and point out sin. A New Covenant prophet will not violate New Covenant values as they prophesy.

_____

_____

_____

_____

_____

_____

_____

_____

_____

_____

How can I operate as a prophet?

Ephesians 4 states that a prophet is given to the church to operate as one of five leaders in the church. Know that if you are called as a prophet by Jesus, you cannot operate in this role until your church leadership sees you as a prophet <u>and</u> releases you to operate in this role. You will be able to operate as a prophet to the extent that your church leadership gives you permission. They will define what this looks like. Remember the principle of submission to leadership is operable here. Choose to submit to the leaders that God has placed within your church.

Be cautious of people who name themselves a prophet and seem to be independent of a biblical community and are not submitted to leadership. God values the body of Christ and desires us to be in relationship operating together (Eph. 4:1-16). You notice that Ephesians 4 lists five groups of people that build up the body of Christ – not just the prophets in isolation.

If Jesus has called you as a prophet, it is unwise to announce this to others. Share this only with trusted friends. If Jesus wants you to operate as a prophet in your church, he will give you favor with the leadership, and they will promote you to the role and function of a prophet. Avoid self-promotion. Recognize that you may be called as a prophet, but if your church does not recognize you in this role or there is no structure within your church for a prophet, you cannot operate as one. As prophetic people, it is vital that we remain in submission to our church leadership and operate in our prophetic gift or in our role as prophets as our leadership deems best.

(If this is a topic that interests you and you would like to study the topic of prophets further, I highly recommend reading <u>School of the Prophets</u> by Kris Vallotton. Kris Vallotton offers a balanced view of what prophets are, but also what they are not. He provides foundation teaching on this topic and critical advanced training.)

Listening Exercise

Line Prophesying

After this activity, on your own, take notes to remember any prophetic
words that impacted you.

_____

_____

_____

_____

_____

_____

_____

_____

_____

_____

_____

_____

_____

_____

Going Deeper–Extra Practice

Treasure Box

(If you have read "Deeper – Heart to Heart with Holy Spirit" and have done the listening exercise of the Treasure Box then you will know what to expect for this activity. In this exercise you will be placing different names in the box.)

Once people begin to operate in their gift of prophecy, I consistently hear them say how difficult it is to prophesy over people that they know well. As you receive information from Holy Spirit about a friend or family member, it is easy to second guess yourself and question, 'Is this Holy Spirit, or am I just thinking this because I know the person so well?' This Going Deeper exercise is similar to the Listening Exercise this week and will help you receive a prophetic word for people you know well.

Think of all the people within your Deeper prophetic group. Write each of their names on separate, small pieces of paper and place them in a small box. Pick a name out of the box. Without looking at who you have picked, begin to ask Holy Spirit questions about the person and write a prophetic word for them. Once you are finished writing, look at the name that you have picked.

Process with Holy Spirit:

- Does this word 'fit' the person?
- Seek Holy Spirit as to what to do with the word:
  - Does he want you to use this to pray for the person?
  - Does he want you to give it to the person? If 'yes', ask him when the timing would be good. If he does not want you to give it to the person, ask him what to do with the word.

Repeat this process as often as you like.

Deeper - Part Two

ENCOUNTER SESSION 10
How To Give A Prophetic Word To Others

The Eagle has Landed

"I, JESUS, HAVE SENT MY ANGEL TO GIVE YOU THIS TESTIMONY FOR THE CHURCHES. I AM THE ROOT AND THE OFFSPRING OF DAVID, AND THE BRIGHT MORNING STAR." REVELATION 22:16 (NIV)

THE EAGLE IN THIS PICTURE REPRESENTS THE GIFT OF PROPHECY. THE GIFT OF PROPHECY HOLDS THE KEY TO UNLOCKING MYSTERIES AND TREASURES IN HEAVEN FROM GOD. JESUS (REPRESENTED BY THE BRIGHT MORNING STAR) IS OUR HIGH PRIEST AND IS PRAYING FOR GOD'S WILL TO BE ACCOMPLISHED IN OUR LIVES. THE GIFT OF PROPHECY FLOWS OUT OF JESUS' HEART FOR US AND SPEAKS TRUTH, HOPE, AND LOVE. THE EAGLE HAS LANDED IS AN EXPRESSION USED WHEN SOMETHING HAS BEEN ACCOMPLISHED. MY HOPE AND DESIRE IS THAT THE GIFT OF PROPHECY WILL FLOW FREELY AND PURELY THROUGH GOD'S PEOPLE.

WWW.DEANNASDECORATIVEDESIGNS.CA
ORIGINAL ACRYLIC PAINTINGS AND PRINTS BY
DEANNA OELKE

Worship Reflections

Journal, Draw, Doodle

Deeper—Encounter Session 10
How to Give a Prophetic Word to Others

"The one who prophesies speaks to people for their strengthening, encouraging and comfort." (1 Cor. 14:3 NIV)

As God begins to speak to you and show you things about another person, you will need to process the information that he is giving to you, and then decide how to deliver it. This can involve multitasking as you may be receiving from the Lord as you are speaking the word to the person. The whole process of receiving and delivering a word becomes easier with practice. Also, do not expect that Holy Spirit will give you a prophetic word in the same way each time. Be open to however he may want to show you something for another person.

1. Receiving a prophetic word from the Lord

God may choose to invade your space and give you a prophetic word for someone. God can do this in the following ways:

- A thought about a person that randomly comes into your mind.
- An impression or a feeling about a person.
- God being more obvious and saying, "I want to talk to you about someone."
- Be sensitive to his voice and any other way that he may want to speak to you.

Instead of dismissing the subtler ways that God desires to give you a prophetic word, engage with God and begin to dialogue with him about the information. When you are aware that God is giving you a word for someone else, ask him, "Do you want me to speak this out now, later or never?" Do not assume that because God is showing you something that you have to speak it out immediately. Be patient, and be sensitive to God's timing.

If God is showing you something negative about a person, ask him how he wants you to present it. Remember to only speak out words that will strengthen, encourage and comfort. God may be showing you something about another person so that you can pray for them; he may not want you to speak out the prophetic word. Be obedient as the Lord directs you.

Once you have the gift of prophecy you can also invade God's space and receive a prophetic word for nearly anyone. When you begin to ask the Lord for prophetic words for others you may find it easier to begin by asking him a question (see examples in the Going Deeper Listening Exercise at the end of this chapter). Once you become more practiced, you simply will be able to ask God, "What would you like to say to this person?" This will be enough of a lead in for him to begin giving you information.

_____

_____

_____

_____

_____

_____

_____

_____

_____

_____

_____

_____

2. Expanding the prophetic word

As you begin to receive from the Holy Spirit, continue to ask him questions. Ask him what the word means, what he is saying to this person, and if there is anything more he wants to show you. Ensure that you receive all of the information that Holy Spirit desires to give you.

If you are trying to expand on the prophetic words, and you are not getting more than one word, sentence or simple picture, begin to speak out what you see. Often God will give more once you start speaking; sometimes the step of faith often unfolds the 'more' of the word. This requires more boldness on your part. Then, as you are speaking, multitask and continue to ask God questions as you are speaking. You may be listening to God and speaking to the person at the same time.

If you speak out the one word and don't receive any more from Holy Spirit, then trust that he desired to give you a simple message to deliver to the person. You can present a simple prophetic word like this: "I am just hearing the word 'boldness' for you. I am not sure what else God wants to say regarding this. Maybe you can ask the Lord what he desires to say." I find at times that the simple prophetic words are remembered the easiest and sometimes have more impact than multiple sentences. Remember that even one single spoken word from the heart of God can accomplish exactly what he desires (Is. 55:11).

Sometimes as I am receiving a prophetic word, I can sense that there is more to the prophetic word, but I cannot access more. Holy Spirit seems to be withholding information from me. In these moments, I will tell the person that I sense that there is more to the prophetic word, and I then encourage them to journey with Holy Spirit to discover more information and details.

_____

_____

_____

_____

_____

3. Delivering the prophetic word

Be mindful of your environment, and be culturally relevant in how you present your prophetic word from the Lord. Is this person a Christian? If they are a Christian, is hearing from the Lord part of their 'normal'? Present the word in a way that they will be able to receive it. Christians may not be familiar with the prophetic. You may choose to stay away from words like prophecy/prophetic until you know what their understanding is.

If the person is a Christian, you may say something like this:

- "I sense that God is telling me something encouraging for you, is it okay if I share it with you?"

If they are not a Christian, think of how you may present it:

- "I am a Christian (or follower of Jesus), and I believe that God still speaks to people today. I feel like he was telling me some encouraging things about you. May I share them with you?"

I have found that it is important as you lead into giving a prophetic word to say somewhere in your introduction that you have something encouraging to share with them. I discovered this as I would approach people by saying, "I sense that God is showing me something about you." I could tell from their shocked and terrified expression that they were thinking that God had shown me something bad about them or some sin. They were thinking in Old Covenant prophecy guidelines, not New Covenant. With a simple introduction and using the word 'encouraging' you will be easing God's people into New Covenant prophetic values.

Sometimes the person's belief system will keep them from receiving the word. Some people do not believe that God speaks today and they do not believe in the gift of prophecy. Sometimes you cannot be aware of this before you give a prophetic word.

If the person does not respond positively towards you, do not become discouraged.   Bless them anyway.   Keep being obedient as the Lord prompts to share encouraging prophetic words with others.

_____

_____

_____

_____

_____

_____

_____

4. Releasing Prophetic Words

Your words should push people into God.   We want people to be dependent on God, not us. Think of how you can end your prophetic word so that you very simply can tell them the 'next steps':

- "Take these words to the Lord and see what he says about it."

With a statement like this you are communicating that God desires to speak to them personally, that they have access to God, what they can do next, and that you are not the expert on their life – God is.

Once you have delivered a prophetic word, your job is probably done. You now release others in their journey. People will have varied responses to your prophetic words. By giving prophetic words I have made new friends, journeyed deeply with people, scared people who were afraid of what I would 'see', and offended those who could not receive the word. Whatever the response, process with Holy Spirit after to have him be your teacher regarding your delivery. Holy Spirit may have you continue to pray for the person as he reminds you. Be faithful to pray for them with his prompts and continue to engage with them in providing prophetic words if Holy Spirit desires you to.

Many times you will not know if your prophetic words came to pass. This can be hard. This is where you need to engage faith and trust that Holy Spirit will continue to work in their life to accomplish all that he desires. Not seeing the fulfillment of some of your prophetic words is another reason why prophetic community is so important. You need to see in people's lives if your prophetic words are bearing fruit. Remember that sometimes fruit grows with time. You may only see the fulfillment of your prophetic words if you are journeying with people over time. Your prophetic words should be bearing fruit; there should be some people in your life that you are able to track your prophetic words with.

5. Prophetic words to avoid

I think it is wise to take some time to touch on prophetic words to avoid. I sometimes come across people who are reluctant to the prophetic because they have been hurt through those not stewarding their gift well. Often they have been hurt by someone who is not operating in New Covenant values, and sin was pointed out, or they felt judged. However, sometimes the content of the prophetic word was hurtful.

- **Avoid prophetic words that give direction to a person's future.**

Words should not be <u>specifically</u> directive (ex: God wants you to quit your job and move to Africa). You may have a sense of a direction that God wants to take them. If this is the case, present the prophetic word in a way that the person needs to press into God to receive the specific direction.

  - "I sense that there is something related to traveling. Ask the Lord more about this and what this looks like. Trust his leading and his timing."

- **Avoid prophetic words that give dates, mates or predict babies.**

You can well imagine that prophetic words that predict a timeline, someone's mate or predict the birth of a baby can be very hurtful if you are wrong. It is wise to stay away from words of this nature.

_____

_____

_____

_____

_____

_____

_____

_____

Listening Exercise

Collective Prophesying

When you are prophesying over one person in a group, often it will feel like building a jigsaw puzzle together. One person will get a sense and speak out one part of what God wants to say, then another person will add to the previous word and maybe expand it, and so on until the full prophetic word is built. The exercises this week will build on this idea and will go along with the biblical principle that we are to take turns when prophesying (1 Cor. 14:31).

Bible Character:

1. Sit your group in a circle. Everyone will start with a piece of paper. You do not know who you are prophesying over, so you need to rely completely on Holy Spirit. Holy Spirit knows which prophetic word is for you and which one you are going to receive.
2. Each individual person asks the Lord for a character from the Bible. Write the character at the top of the page. Then ask the Lord to bring something from the Bible character to mind. And ask God what he would like to say to the person that will be receiving this prophetic word. Encourage your people to keep their written words 2-3 sentences long.
3. Pass the paper to the person to the left, so that everyone has a new paper. Read what the previous person has written, and ask God what else he would like to say. Write only 2-3 sentences.
4. Pass the paper to the left again, and repeat the process.
5. Do this a number of times.
6. Collect the papers and randomly pass them out. The paper you receive is your prophetic word. Process with the Lord, and then share with the group.

Going Deeper–Extra Practice

Prophetic Practice

As you become more familiar with your prophetic gift, practice using it at your initiative. Don't just wait for Holy Spirit to invade your space and give you a word for others. Invade his space, and get a prophetic word for someone!

The following are simple questions to ask Father God, Jesus, or Holy Spirit to receive a prophetic word for others:

- Where are you Jesus?

Whether you are interacting with one person or in a group of people, Jesus is present. As you engage with him and ask him questions, this often can be a precursor into a prophetic word. Begin to ask Jesus 'where are you in the room?' If you sense that he is interacting with a particular person, begin to ask him questions about this interaction - what he wants to do in the person's life. Ask him if there is anything that he wants to say to this person. Process with Jesus, and practice presenting prophetic words to others within your family, friends, and others outside of your Deeper group. Remember to present your word in a way that will be received by your audience.

- What do you love about this person?
- What about this person makes you smile?
- What Bible verse is particularly significant for them in this season of their life?

Deeper – Part Two

ENCOUNTER SESSION 11
Celebration & Prophetic Words

"YAHWEH! THE LORD! THE GOD OF COMPASSION AND MERCY! I AM SLOW TO ANGER AND FILLED WITH UNFAILING LOVE AND FAITHFULNESS."
EXODUS 34:6

WHAT WOULD IT LOOK LIKE IF YOU LIVED YOUR LIFE AS AN ACT OF WORSHIP WITH COMPLETE ABANDON IN THE LOVE OF FATHER GOD? FATHER IS GOOD, HE IS LOVING, AND HE IS FULL OF KINDNESS AND MERCY. HE IS CALLING YOU TO TRUST HIM WITH ALL OF WHO YOU ARE. STEP INTO HIS LOVE WITH ABANDON!

WWW.DEANNASDECORATIVEDESIGNS.CA
ORIGINAL ACRYLIC PAINTINGS AND PRINTS BY
DEANNA OELKE

Worship Reflections

Journal, Draw, Doodle

Deeper—Encounter Session 11

Celebration & Prophetic Words

Record the prophetic word that you receive and/or take notes:

_____

_____

_____

_____

_____

_____

_____

_____

_____

_____

_____

_____

_____

_____

_____

Deeper - Part Two

ENCOUNTER SESSION 12
How To Steward Prophetic Words Others Have Given You

Glory Mountain

"COME, LET US GO TO THE MOUNTAIN OF THE LORD, TO THE HOUSE OF THE GOD OF JACOB. HE WILL TEACH US HIS WAYS, SO THAT WE MAY WALK IN HIS PATHS." MICAH 4:2

I PAINTED THIS PICTURE DURING WORSHIP AT A CONFERENCE. I WANTED TO SHOW THAT WE NEED TO BE LIKE CHILDREN TO ENTER THE KINGDOM OF HEAVEN. THE SWORD IN HIS HAND REPRESENTS THE SWORD OF THE SPIRIT—THE WORD OF THE LORD. TO FOLLOW THE PATH IS OUR CHOICE. THERE IS A DOOR IN THE MOUNTAIN THAT LEADS INTO THE PRESENCE OF THE LORD. THERE IS A SMALL HERALDING ANGEL IN THE CLOUDS, RELEASING A CLARION CALL TO ALL BELIEVERS.

WWW.DEANNASDECORATIVEDESIGNS.CA
ORIGINAL ACRYLIC PAINTINGS AND PRINTS BY
DEANNA OELKE

Worship Reflections

Journal, Draw, Doodle

Deanna's Reflections on Stewarding Personal Prophetic Words

At this point in your Deeper journey, you have multiple prophetic words that have been spoken over you. You might be thinking, 'What do I do with these now?' This week you will learn some tools to help you in knowing what the next steps could be.

Before we begin to talk about how to journey with prophetic words and the spoken word of God (prophecies or Holy Spirit's voice directly to you), let's talk about how you journey with the written word of God - the Bible. There are times when you hear or read a Bible verse, and it seems to leap off of the page. You feel the truth of what you read, and you experience the Bible as the active and living word of God doing a work in your spirit even as you are hearing it. Your part is simply to submit to God and receive the truth as it floods your spirit. Then there are times that you read a Bible verse that is a promise of God like: "God causes everything to work together for the good of those who love God and are called according to his purpose for them." (Romans 8:28). You know that this is truth, but your situation in that moment of your life is not good, and you may be experiencing the reality of the enemy stealing from you and destroying parts of you (Jn. 10:10).

How do you respond when the truth of God's written word does not line up with the fact of your life?

- You choose to engage faith and continue to believe that what God has said in the Bible is truth and is true for you.
- You trust in God and his character - that he is good, that he loves you, and that he is for you not against you.
- You trust in God's timing for your life, and that he has a plan for the larger vision of your life. (Jer. 29:11)
- You pray in cooperation for the truth of God's word to be manifested in your life.
- You choose to set your sights on God, and renew your mind in the promises of God.

Journeying with prophetic words compared to the spoken word of God has some similarities but also some differences.

One of the main differences in stewarding prophetic words compared to stewarding Bible verses is how you 'hold' the word. Let me explain. The Bible is truth. When God says in the Bible that he will work all things together for good for those who love him and are called according to his purpose for them (Rom. 8:28), you know that this is truth. You can go boldly before his throne of grace with confidence saying, "God, I love you and I am called according to your purpose for me, so I am asking you to touch this situation in my life. You said that you will work all things together for good, so I am asking you to turn this current situation in my life into something good. Thank you!" God cannot deny himself, and he cannot go against his written word. You can hold the promises in his written word tightly, with a closed hand, and cling to them as truth. Prophecy can be truth as well, but prophecy should be held loosely with an open hand.

One of the main truths that you need to remember in stewarding the spoken word of God is that prophecy is partial information (1 Cor. 13:9). Prophecy is one puzzle piece and not the whole picture. When you first hear a prophetic word that is visionary and for the future, you will probably have an idea as to how it will work out in your life. God often has a unique and sometimes very different way of working out a word in our lives. God's ways are not our ways (Isa. 55:8). We can do our part to move ourselves towards a prophetic word from the Lord, but there is always an element of letting go and trusting God to do his part and to move in his way and his time. Don't control and manipulate circumstances in your life to force a prophetic word to happen. Do your part, and then step back and give God room to do the miraculous in your life!

Deanna

...deep calls to deep...
Psalm 42:7

Deeper—Encounter Session 12
How to Steward Prophetic Words Others Have Given to You

As you have been giving prophetic words to others, you have ensured that the prophetic words you deliver are encouraging, strengthening and comforting. As well, ensure that prophetic words that others speak over you are in line with this spiritual principle. Do not allow others that are prophesying to point out your sin or tell you what you are doing wrong. Set good boundaries for yourself. If someone begins to point out sin or you are feeling the word is discouraging stop them and say something like this, "Can you stop please. I believe that the gift of prophecy is for the encouragement, strengthening and comfort of God's people. I am not feeling encouraged by your prophetic word, and I am not interested in hearing anymore." Ensure that you are just receiving prophetic words that are encouraging. Remember that you are responsible for stewarding prophetic words that others have given you. Take every encouraging word to Holy Spirit to ask him what he would like to say to you regarding the word.

If you haven't started already, consider writing down what Holy Spirit is speaking to you and prophetic words that you receive from others. Writing down the words will keep you from forgetting them and will also help you in easily reviewing what the Lord has said. Consider the following as you are reviewing your prophetic words with the Lord:

1. **Prophecy must be weighed. Test prophecy with scripture, the character of God, and share your word with trusted prophetic friends and leaders for insight and counsel.**

"Do not quench the Spirit. Do not treat prophecies with contempt but test them all; hold on to what is good." (1 Thess. 5:19-21 NIV)

Paul exhorts us to test every prophecy. While every believer can flow in a general grace of the prophetic, we certainly don't walk in an authority of infallibility. Almost everyone has had a situation where we believed that God spoke to us and later we found out that he didn't. Notice that Paul wants us to test everything, not everyone. Test the prophecy against the truth of the Bible and use discernment. Testing a prophetic word involves testing the details. It doesn't have to be an 'all or nothing' approach. Hold onto the parts of the word that are good and leave the rest.

Test the word yourself, but also share your word with others. As you are sharing your words with others, it is important that you share them with people who know you and people who understand prophecy. Ensure that the people that you share your word with will not treat your prophecy with contempt.

Just as you would watch for supernatural fruit when God has spoken to you, watch for supernatural fruit with your prophetic words. Do you feel truth, fruit of the Spirit, life, or hope when you first hear the prophetic word? If you do, this is good fruit. Remember that sometimes the fruit grows with time. This is where writing your prophetic words down is helpful for going back, revisiting and seeing which ones have come to pass or have borne fruit.

2. Prophecy requires us to engage faith.

Does this prophetic word stir a desire within you? Do you want this to happen in your life? If yes, pray in agreement with Holy Spirit for this to happen in your life. Remember that Holy Spirit is praying that the will of Father God will be manifested in your life (Rom. 8:26-27). You may have this desire because Holy Spirit first had this desire for you and placed it in your heart! Sometimes Christians think if they have a desire for God to do something in their lives that this desire is then selfish. That is not necessarily the case. If the prophetic word sparks a desire in your heart, and this desire is in line with scripture, then pray for it to happen. This is not selfish. The reality is that God wants to <u>immeasurably</u> more than you can ask or imagine (Eph. 3:20).

_____

_____

_____

_____

_____

_____

_____

_____

_____

_____

3. Prophecy sometimes requires action on our part.

"Timothy, my son, I am giving you this command in keeping with the prophecies once made about you, so that by recalling them you may fight the battle well." (1 Tim. 1:18 NIV)

Different types of words require different kinds of action:

- A 'now' word: The easiest prophetic words to journey with are the words that are for right now. These are the prophetic words that when you hear them, you feel good supernatural fruit and the truth of the word. Your part is to just receive and allow the word to wash over your spirit and your mind. Allow the word to actively do the work that Holy Spirit desires. In the 'now' words, there is an immediate work that the Lord does that we just need to be open to; there is not much stewardship beyond just receiving from the Lord.

_____

_____

- An identity word: If the prophetic word is a truth about who you are, you can use it in the same way you would 'fight the battle' with a Bible verse: engage your faith and believe that this is truth, even if you can't see it in the natural. Be transformed by the renewing of your mind. Take all of your thoughts captive to the obedience of Christ.

_____

_____

- **A healing word:** You may sense, feel, or hear the healing in a prophetic word. Press into Holy Spirit, Jesus, or Father God to ensure that he completes the work of healing in your life. Is there something more that he wants to say? Is there something that you need to process in the presence of Holy Spirit? Do you need to utilize the principles of combating lies from the enemy (Deeper Encounter Session 4)?

_____

_____

_____

_____

_____

- **A visionary word:** You may receive a word that speaks of things for the future. Is there something that you can do to practically move towards this prophetic word for it to happen? If so, engage with Holy Spirit and make a plan and begin to take steps forward. You will probably have an idea of how this future word could unfold in your life. Remember that God's ways are not our ways (Isa. 55:8). Do your part, stay tuned in to Holy Spirit and allow God to do his part in the way that he wants to.

_____

_____

_____

_____

_____

4. Prophecy is partial information.

"For we know in part and we prophesy in part." (1 Cor. 13:9 NIV)

Do not make any major decisions on one prophetic blessing alone. If you have a prophetic word that points to making a major decision, ask the Lord for more information, ask for his timing, ask for confirmation and seek out wise counsel from others.

_____

_____

_____

_____

5. Prophecy sometimes takes time; patiently wait for it.

"For the revelation awaits an appointed time; it speaks of the end and will not prove false. Though it lingers, wait for it; it will certainly come and will not delay." (Hab. 2:3 NIV)

Waiting can be hard, especially when you are excited about something! Sometimes God fulfills a prophetic word more slowly than what we want or expect. God is outside of time and is very patient. Sometimes he may choose to fulfill a prophetic word on the other side of eternity - when we die and enter heaven. Trust God, trust his ways, and trust his timing.

_____

_____

_____

_____

What if a prophetic word never happens?

The emotional journey of a prophetic word not being fulfilled can be difficult, especially if it is something that you have desired, hoped for and prayed for. If you choose love and relationship with the Trinity your goal as you journey with a prophetic word, instead of the fulfillment of the prophetic word, then you avoid intense disappointment if the word does not come to pass. A prophetic word not happening should not jeopardize your relationship with God. If an unfulfilled word does negatively affect your relationship with God, then there is a problem in where you are placing your hope. Our hope should be placed in the Lord first.

Let us consider some possible reasons as to why words may not come to pass:

- There is a human factor in prophetic words; we are not perfect. Even though the word may be encouraging, the person prophesying may have communicated information that was from him/herself. Good people can deliver incorrect words; an incorrect word does not mean that the person is 'bad'. Remember that 1 Thess. 5:19-21 encourages us to test prophetic words, not prophetic people.

- Sometimes a prophetic word is active just for a season. Other people may need to cooperate for the word to happen, or there was action on your part that was necessary. If you feel you may have missed an opportunity with the Lord, ask him for another chance. Our God is full of grace.

- Sometimes God allows a prophetic promise to die in order that it may produce more seeds in our lives and a fruitful harvest (Jn. 12:24). God is not necessarily finished with the word yet! Put the word aside and ask God to let you know when you are supposed to engage with it again.

- Sometimes it is more important to God to show us our priorities than to fulfill a prophetic word. Above everything, we are to desire God first. As you move forward into a prophetic word that you dearly want to happen in your life, what if at the end of the journey all you have is God? Is having God enough for you? God desires to be first in your life.

- Sometimes God is more concerned about the journey than the word being fulfilled. Sometimes God desires to grow character within us. Sometimes there are details about ourselves that he wants to reveal. Submit the whole process to God not only the end result.

In journeying with any prophetic words, your default should always be following the lead of Holy Spirit. He is your guide and your companion. Trust him and how he is working out everything for your good.

_____

_____

_____

_____

_____

_____

_____

_____

_____

_____

_____

Listening Exercise

Processing Your Prophetic Word

_____

_____

_____

_____

_____

_____

_____

_____

_____

_____

_____

_____

_____

_____

<u>Going Deeper–Extra Practice</u>

Prophetic words in the past few weeks have been focused on receiving words quickly and speaking out words even as we are receiving them from the Lord. Practicing words in this way prepares us for randomly giving strangers a prophetic word or giving a friend a word as we are having a conversation with them. Sometimes you may be on your own, the Lord brings someone to your mind and begins to press them on your heart. He wants you to do something: he wants you to give them a message from his heart. The Extra Practice exercise this week will give you practice in what you can do when this happens.

You will journey with the Lord regarding the person whose name you picked. Ask the Lord to bring this person to mind as he wants you to pray for them. Ask Holy Spirit what he is praying for them. Send your 'person' texts or e-mails as you receive things from the Lord for them.

Try to send them 1-2 prophetic words per week. If you like, spoil them and send them words more often!

Deeper - Part Two

ENCOUNTER SESSION 13
Words of Wisdom and Words of Knowledge

"BLESSED ARE THE POOR IN SPIRIT, FOR THEIRS IS THE KINGDOM OF HEAVEN." MATTHEW 5:3 (NIV)

THIS YOUNG LADY SEES HER NEED OF GOD; SHE IS COMING WITH EMPTY HANDS, READY TO RECEIVE GOD. SHE KNOWS THAT WHEN SHE SEEKS GOD, SHE WILL FIND HIM. SHE HAS ONE GOAL—TO LOVE HER GOD WITH ALL OF HER HEART, SOUL AND MIND. GOD IS REPRESENTED IN HER HANDS WITH THE TRINITY SYMBOL. THE KINGDOM OF GOD FLOWS OUT OF THIS DIVINE INTERACTION— REPRESENTED BY THE SYMBOLISM OF THE BUTTERFLIES, FEATHERS, AND THE JEWELS.

WWW.DEANNASDECORATIVEDESIGNS.CA
ORIGINAL ACRYLIC PAINTINGS AND PRINTS BY
DEANNA OELKE

Kingdom of Heaven

<u>Worship Reflections</u>

Journal, Draw, Doodle

Deanna's Reflections on Words of Wisdom and Words of Knowledge

"Now to each one the manifestation of the Spirit is given for the common good. To one there is given through the Spirit a <u>message of wisdom</u>, to another a <u>message of knowledge</u> by means of the same Spirit," (1 Cor. 12:7-8)

The message of wisdom, and message of knowledge are gifts from Holy Spirit that complement the gift of prophecy. A word (or message) of wisdom is supernatural wisdom that comes from Holy Spirit not your own mind or your natural wisdom. A word (or message) of knowledge is information about the person that there is no way that you could know by yourself. Holy Spirit gives you supernatural knowledge and information.

As I began to grow in my gift of prophecy, Holy Spirit began to give me words of knowledge and words of wisdom. I began to see how beautifully words of knowledge, prophecy, and words of wisdom would flow together and provide a full message. It could have been easy for me to try and operate in all three gifts each time I was to prophesy. I choose to remain in the simplicity of following Holy Spirit's lead and allowing him to form the prophetic word and the ministry as he desired. Holy Spirit knows what is best for the person to hear.

Words of Wisdom:
There is a richness in wisdom from heaven. I remember when I began to receive words of wisdom. I knew that it was the gift of wisdom because the wisdom did not come from my knowledge or from my experience.
It was supernatural! Often when I receive a word of wisdom, my reaction is: "This is good!" I often find that I learn from the word of wisdom as much as the person that I am speaking to.

Words of Knowledge:

Words of knowledge can be showy. They carry a factor of: "Wow, how did you know that about me?" Ensure that your focus is on the work that Holy Spirit wants to do in the person you are ministering to and Christ within you. Choose to operate in love and humility.

When I receive a word of knowledge about a person, I press in to Holy Spirit to find out how he wants me to use the information and if he wants me to speak it out. I remember one time being invited into a Bible study with a group of ladies that I did not know. At the end of the study, we were moving into a time of prophesying over each other. One particular lady was to receive prophetic words. As I was asking Holy Spirit what he wanted to say, I immediately had a vision of her being abused by men. I knew that I could not speak out the rawness of what I saw; I thought that it could be embarrassing for this to be revealed to the group. I pressed deep into Holy Spirt to receive wisdom in the delivery. This is what he told me to say, "God knows that you have not been treated well by men in the past (the word of knowledge graciously communicated). Jesus wants to reveal himself as a gentleman to you (the prophetic message)." The prophetic word then carried a word of wisdom as to how she could practically engage with Jesus to position herself to learn from him as the gentleman. This lady needed to know that God saw the hurt of her past, he cared for her, and he now wanted to heal her through Jesus.

I remember another time I was teaching a small group of young girls how to hear God's voice. As we began listening to God for each other, I saw for one girl a vision of Jesus bouncing like Tigger (the tiger in Winnie the Pooh). I could have very easily dismissed this as my crazy imagination and waited for something serious from Holy Spirit. I decided to speak out what I saw, and this is what unfolded:

"I see Jesus bouncing like Tigger."

The girls all gasped and looked at each other - their eyes wide. I knew that something was up; God was somehow in that seemingly silly vision. The girls quickly told me that earlier that evening when the girls were talking amongst themselves, this girl had said that her friends nicknamed her 'Tigger'. God had their attention. I then had the interpretation to the vision and knew why Jesus looked like Tigger.

"Jesus knows you so perfectly, and he wants to relate to you in a way that you will understand."

A word of wisdom then came as to how she could practically engage with Jesus to allow him to reveal himself to her very personally.

I hope and pray that as you journey with Holy Spirit and as you conform more and more to the likeness of Jesus, you will be a prophetic voice of love, hope, truth and healing for the world, and for the body of Christ.

Deanna

...deep calls to deep...
Psalm 42:7

Deeper—Encounter Session 13

Words of Wisdom & Words of Knowledge

Gifts of Holy Spirit that complement the gift of prophecy

Holy Spirit is so extravagant! You may find that as you simply exercise your gift of prophecy that Holy Spirit begins to give you other gifts. We will be specifically focusing on the gifts of Holy Spirit that complement the gift of prophecy: words of wisdom and words of knowledge. In our Deeper teaching, the teaching around these gifts will be practical in nature. The focus will remain on the gift of prophecy and how words of wisdom and words of knowledge compliment the gift of prophecy.

"Now to each one the manifestation of the Spirit is given for the common good. To one there is given through the Spirit a <u>message of wisdom</u>, to another a <u>message of knowledge</u> by means of the same Spirit." (1 Cor. 12:7-8 NIV)

1. A message/word of wisdom:

Definition: Supernatural wisdom versus human or worldly wisdom; seeing life from God's perspective. The gift of wisdom is the application of knowledge that God gives you.

"But the wisdom from above is first of all pure. It is also peace loving, gentle at all times, and willing to yield to others. It is full of mercy and the fruit of good deeds. It shows no favoritism and is always sincere." (Jas. 3:17)

The benefit of this gift with the gift of prophecy: Where a word of knowledge opens up a person's spirit and the gift of prophecy provides a message, a word of wisdom can give instruction as to what to do next. It is a supernatural perspective to know the means for accomplishing God's will in a given situation. This gift could involve having a sense of divine direction, being led by the Holy Spirit to act appropriately, and/or rightly applying knowledge. You will know when you are given a message of wisdom because it does not come from your experiences or what you know. Often a word of wisdom will even teach you in the situation. The Bible speaks so much about the benefit of wisdom. Eagerly desire this gift, and pray for wisdom as you see that you need it.

_____

_____

_____

_____

_____

_____

2. A message/word of knowledge:

Definition: Supernatural insight or understanding by revelation. This is information that you could not have received on you own; God gives you this information.

Biblical examples:

- Ananias in the conversion of Paul (Acts 9:10-12)
- Cornelius in finding Peter, who then was instrumental in bringing the Holy Spirit to the Gentiles (Acts 10)

The benefit of this gift with the gift of prophecy: This gift works very well with the gift of prophecy. A message of supernatural knowledge communicates to the person, "God sees you!" Often a message of knowledge opens up a person's spirit, so that there are no walls or defence mechanisms. A prophetic word then communicating the truth and the love of Father God for the person is powerful.

The message of knowledge, like the gift of prophecy, can be practiced. Firstly, pray for this gift. As you interact with a person, ask Holy Spirit for information that you could only know from him. Then ask the person questions to find out if the information is accurate. Let me explain. You are at a gathering of people, and you are interacting with a woman that you do not know very well. As you ask Holy Spirit about a word of knowledge, you sense that she has a son that plays basketball. Begin then to ask the lady questions to find out if you have indeed received a word of knowledge from Holy Spirit: "Do you have children? Does your son play sports? What kind of sports does he play?" The purpose of practicing with words of knowledge is not to minister, or prophesy, but for you to grow in your gift. As you begin to see that you are moving in the gift of word of knowledge, you will begin to step out in faith and boldness.

_____

_____

_____

_____

As you are prophesying, you may naturally begin to move in the gifts of message of wisdom and message of knowledge. The essence of prophesying is simply following Holy Spirit's lead. Be sensitive to how he is leading you, and process with Holy Spirit even as you are delivering a word.

Listening Exercise

Practicing Words of Knowledge

Write down any prophetic words and words of knowledge that you want to remember from this exercise.

_____

_____

_____

_____

_____

_____

_____

_____

_____

_____

Going Deeper–Extra Practice

Continue to practice using the gift of knowledge. Try getting words of knowledge for friends or people that you don't know very well. With the practice of receiving, processing and then delivering words from the Lord readily, try applying this practice in the world. Try asking the Lord for strangers. Remember to be culturally relevant as you are presenting the word.

Deeper - Part Two

ENCOUNTER SESSION 14
Glory Stories

Alabaster Jar

"Then she knelt behind him at his feet, weeping. Her tears fell on his feet, and she wiped them off with her hair. Then she kept kissing his feet and putting perfume on them." Luke 7:38

I WAS INSPIRED TO PAINT JULIE MEYER'S SONG ALABASTER BOX. IN THIS SONG SHE SINGS ABOUT GIVING ALL THAT SHE HAS, JUST AS MARY OF BETHANY DID IN BREAKING THE ALABASTER BOX AT THE FEET OF JESUS. AS I LISTEN TO THIS SONG, I OFTEN IMAGINE WHAT THE DIFFERENT FRAGRANCES OF MY OFFERINGS TO JESUS WOULD LOOK LIKE. THIS IS THE IDEA THAT I TRIED TO CAPTURE IN THIS PAINTING.

WWW.DEANNASDECORATIVEDESIGNS.CA
ORIGINAL ACRYLIC PAINTINGS AND PRINTS BY
DEANNA OELKE

Worship Reflections

Journal, Draw, Doodle

Deeper—Encounter Session 14

Glory Stories

As you are leaving the Deeper Encounter Sessions it is up to you as to how you will foster your prophetic gift. You are responsible for the growth and stewardship of your gift.

Here are some ideas to help you continue to grow:

- **Practice hearing God's voice for yourself and others.**

  - Faithfully steward what the Lord is giving you. Act on what he shows you.

- **Ask the Lord for increase.**

  - "You do not have, because you do not ask God." (Jas. 4:2)
  - Ask and be open to God revealing himself in new ways.

- **Hang out with those who love the prophetic.**

  - Learn from those who know and practice the gift of prophecy, and build relationships with them. It is wise to be a part of the body of Christ as this is who the gift of prophecy is for. Do not isolate yourself.

- **Seek out opportunities within your church to use your prophetic gift.**

Listening Exercise

Glory Stories

Record any prophetic words that you receive this session

_____

_____

_____

_____

_____

_____

_____

_____

_____

_____

_____

_____

About the Author

Deanna Oelke

I grew up in a Baptist home, and was raised by parents that lived their Christian life authentically. This strong biblical upbringing was foundational for my Christian maturity and for Holy Spirit to lead me into my spiritual gifts. As an adult, I learned how to hear God's voice for myself. Within a small community of Christian women, I received the gift of prophecy from Holy Spirit. We met weekly and practiced listening to God and prophesying to each other. I experienced Holy Spirit as my personal mentor, teacher, guide and counsellor. After being in this community for a number of months I experienced dramatic spiritual growth, transformation and inner healing.

This experience of prophetic community motivated my friend and I to create a prophetic ministry. We taught men, women and children how to hear God's voice for themselves and others, and how to steward the gift of prophecy. Within our community and prophetic culture, our people experienced an enriched relationship with God and dynamic spiritual transformation.

Eventually, God led me to re-integrate into established Christian institutions. Leading Deeper communities is one way that God has provided opportunities for me to equip Christians in hearing God's voice, to operate in the gift of prophecy and to equip leaders in creating prophetic communities.

My prayer is that you will experience true biblical community within Deeper. I pray that you may come to know practically, and through experience, the love of Christ which far surpasses mere knowledge; that you may be made complete with all the fullness of life and power that comes from God. My hope is that God will accomplish infinitely more than you might ask or imagine! (Eph. 3:18-20)

Deanna

...deep calls to deep...

Psalm 42:7

Appendix

Additional Resources

There are so many books and resources on prophecy. If you are interested in deepening your knowledge on the subject, I would suggest the following authors:

Graham Cooke is one of my favorite authors. If you are interested in have a good book on the gift of prophecy I would recommend: <u>Approaching the Heart of Prophecy.</u> Graham's soaking CD's are wonderful as well. His website is <u>brilliantbookhouse.com</u>

Kris Vallotton is a great teacher. His website has audio teaching, DVDs, books and free podcasts from Bethel Church. His website is <u>kvministries.com</u>

Shawn Bolz is a spiritual adviser, producer, media personality, and minister. He is passionate about seeing individuals and groups learn how to be the best version of themselves. Shawn has been a pioneer in ministry including the prophetic movement since he was in his teens. His focus on having a genuine relationship with God, creativity through entertainment, and social justice have brought him around the world to meet with churches, CEO's, entertainers, and world leaders. His website is <u>bolzministries.com</u>

Streams Ministries is a great equipping ministry. Founded by John Paul Jackson, Streams Ministries is an in-depth training ministry that exists to nurture individuals in the art of hearing God, dreams, visions and the realms of the supernatural. They seek to mentor those with revelatory gifts so they might grow in deeper intimacy with God. Good books and courses are offered on-line from their websites streamscanada.com and streamsministries.com

Inner Healing: Ellel Ministries is a non-denominational Christian ministry that began in England in 1986 and is now established in over 20 countries around the world. They look to serve the Body of Christ in two main ways - by offering personal prayer ministry to those in need and by training and equipping people so that they can help others more effectively. Their website is ellel.org

WATCH FOR DEANNA'S NEW BOOK!

Deeper – Heart to Heart with Holy Spirit is Deanna Oelke's personal journey from emotional bondage into healing and wholeness in Jesus Christ. Learning to hear the voice of Holy Spirit and being a part of a community that could hear God's voice for others through the gift of prophecy was instrumental in her freedom journey.

This book is ideal for individuals who are interested in learning to hear God's voice for themselves and others through the gift of prophecy. Through this book, Deanna will equip you to practically and personally engage with Holy Spirit, Jesus and Father God through worship experiences and listening to God exercises. Teaching topics will include all of the main teachings of the Deeper group experience covered in Deeper: Hearing God's Voice for Yourself and Others - Leader's Guide and the Participant's Guide.